Who's Who in Henry James

Who's Who
in Henry James

GLENDA LEEMING

TAPLINGER PUBLISHING COMPANY

NEW YORK

First published in the United States in 1976 by
Taplinger Publishing Co., Inc.
New York, New York

Jacket photograph from a portrait by
John Singer Sargent, courtesy of the
National Portrait Gallery, London

Library of Congress Catalog Card Number: LC 75–34783
ISBN 0–8008–8268–7

Contents

Foreword

This is more than a *Who's Who* of the personages in Henry James's twenty novels and his five celebrated *nouvelles*: it can be described as a miniature biographical dictionary. It is 'biographical' even though the people listed originally belonged to Henry James's imagination—and even though the names he artfully gave them are not to be found in any existing registers of births, marriages and deaths. I call the book a dictionary because of the curious power of great novelists to make figments of their imagination (like Scrooge's ghosts) materialise. These acquire permanent shape and character, temperament and passion; they are Tess or Madame Bovary, Anna Karenin or Hans Castorp, Becky Sharp or Pierre. They pass from the creative imagination to the printed page—and from the printed page into the imagination of mankind.

Late in life, Henry James read with delight the 'repertory' of characters in Balzac's *Comédie Humaine* as compiled by MM. Cerfberr and Christophe. Their number and variety— even those who had only walk-on parts—teased the American novelist's mind. Every creature named, he said, in Balzac's 'fictive swarm is in this case preserved to fame; so close is the implication that to have *been* named by such a dispenser of life and privilege is to be, as we say of baronets and peers, created.' James did not, by any means, suggest that these people were created 'real'. They belong to the 'imagined real'. Once imagined, and given verbal existence, they are rarely dislodged from the memory of man. Hester Prynne stands for ever on her Puritan scaffold, or walks in the New England woods proudly wearing her scarlet letter; Oliver Twist is always asking for more; Bazarov is the eternal rebellious son— and who hasn't met the sinewy gentleman with the peaked cap, who lives for ever in Baker Street?

The present compilation puts us into Henry James's world. It is a very particular world; it ranges from Roderick, the young American sculptor in Rome, who feels he has to choose between art and passion to Nick Dormer, who must choose between art and politics, to Hyacinth Robinson who is unable to choose between civilisation and revolution. It is quite proper that these personages be assembled in alphabetical order for our easy reference. No one after reading one of James's more difficult novels, like *The Ambassadors*, would deny the palpability of Madame de Vionnet. We are exposed to her special charm through Lambert Strether's beglamoured vision; we feel we have had a delightful lunch with her on the Left Bank, by the edge of the Seine, with our bottle of straw-coloured Chablis, watching her grey eyes as they move in and out of the talk. As for the unquenchable Daisy, that permanent little American flower of presumptuous girlhood, she has been stepping out of jetliners for years (though she now wears blue jeans) with the same aplomb of the Daisy Miller who once stayed at the *Trois Couronnes* at Vevey and walked in the Pincio in Rome with a vulgar Italian. She remains a poetic essence of the American flirt—as she used to be to an earlier generation of Europeans unaccustomed to the free ways of American girls. And so we might go on to James's gallery of women—to Isabel Archer or Francie Dosson or Nanda or even little Maisie. And then his males—Christopher Newman or Adam Verver, or his Italian Prince with the generic name of all the Americas, Prince Amerigo.

The compiler of this little dictionary has had however a special problem. James was a creator also, in his experimental way, of characters without names. They have to be recorded simply as The Narrator, or The Governess, not to speak of the nameless intellectual key-hole peeper in *The Sacred Fount*. These story-tellers identify themselves by the kind of story they tell and the way in which they tell it. Certain critics call them 'unreliable narrators'. The stories they tell may be unreliable; but the narrators could not be more trustworthy for they characterise themselves with almost unbearable truth. They give themselves away. They are the most credible kind of witness, for they make us party to their wilder imaginings or their 'cool' calculations. James was one of the first of the psychological novelists to show us individuals engaged in their process of self-delusion: the hysterical Governess whose story does not match her own picture of her fortitude; the publishing scoundrel who is proud of his deception of two old women, without understanding his cruelty to them; the prying cross-examining narrator, a comic figure, in the *Fount* who is a mental *voyeur*.

One particular charm resides in this compilation. I refer to the names James chose for his characters. He baptises them freely out of lists compiled in his notebooks from the morning papers. He had a great partiality for names ending in 'er'—Strether, Beever, Dormer, Rover, Striker; and one could add many others from his short stories, John Marcher for example. There are also curious inventions: Mr. Hall Pegg in one short story not listed here, what sort of person was he? James described him privately as 'immense'. And what might we expect from Lord and Lady Wispers? Our *Who's Who* is a guide not only to Jamesian people but to Jamesian nomenclature; and we discover soon enough that these names possess overtones of meaning and suggestion less obviously caricature than Pecksniff or Pickwick, or the Quiverfull of Trollope. One could compile a geographical as well as a biographical dictionary for James since he often invented names of towns in order to be relieved of 'vain specifications'; and it would be an amusing game to try to identify the real country houses of England masquerading as Newmarch or Matcham, Covering End or Summersoft. All sorts of amusing literary sport is thrown up by this fertile little book, put together with loyalty to text and considerable resource and wit. What's in a name? I suspect James would have answered 'everything!'

LEON EDEL

A

ACTON, LIZZIE: A remarkably pretty girl with brilliant eyes and a pert manner: she annoys Eugenia Münster not by rivalry but by seeming indifferent to her. She knows her childhood sweetheart Clifford Wentworth intends to marry her after leaving college, and when he in fact marries her rather earlier, her influence is credited with the settling down that he would have done anyway. *The Europeans*

ACTON, MRS.: Mother of Robert and Lizzie, an emaciated, sweet-faced woman of five-and-fifty, who is very modest, very timid and very ill. Being also very 'intense' she has for her health's sake to limit the visits of the fascinating Eugenia Münster (whose sophistication she embarrasses by direct references to her own approaching death). *The Europeans*

ACTON, ROBERT: A rich American of about forty, with a quick, observant, agreeable dark eye, a small quantity of thin dark hair and a small moustache. He attracts Eugenia Münster, visiting their mutual relations the Wentworths, not only because of his fortune but because of his culture and experience: unlike the Wentworths he has travelled (as far as China) but like them he values pure honesty very highly, and though fascinated by Eugenia, he is repelled by her ambiguous methods and behaviour, however good her motives. Regretting her departure, he nevertheless marries a particularly nice young girl after his mother's death. *The Europeans*

AGGIE (AGNESINA): Niece of the Duchess's dead Neapolitan husband, very beautiful with red hair and a fine complexion, of distinguished ancestry. Brought up on the continental system as innocent and ignorant as possible, with all issues of dangerous importance or complexity kept from her, she is so devoid of ideas as to have almost no character. After marrying Mitchett the shock of freedom impels her to excesses of

I

fast behaviour and Lord Petherton, formerly her aunt's lover, pursues her assiduously. Nanda Brookenham divines that Aggie is trying to find her own character after years of blindness, and recommends Mitchett to help her. *The Awkward Age*

ALDEN, BESSIE: Sister of Mrs. Westgate, a beautiful girl with black hair and blue eyes, brought up in Boston and very thoughtful. Her interest in Lord Lambeth, her sister's guest, and his background is purely sociological but is misconstrued by English observers as fortune hunting, especially during her English holiday. However she ignores hints and warnings from his noble family, and her sudden flight to the Continent is due to the pain of refusing his proposal, not to any social embarrassment. *An International Episode*

ALDERSHAW, LADY: Wife of Lord Aldershaw, she is 'the clever one'. Not young—though denying with every pore that she is old—she is a much bejewelled socialite who tries to capture the successful Milly Theale into her circle and is foiled with polite rudeness by Lord Mark. *The Wings of the Dove*

ALDERSHAW, LORD: A high but slightly stooping, shambling and wavering person who represents urbanity by the liberal aid of certain prominent front teeth. *The Wings of the Dove*

ALMOND, MRS. ELIZABETH: Dr. Sloper's younger and favourite sister, mother of nine children, a comely, comfortable, reasonable woman, cleverer than her sister Lavinia, and more sympathetic than her clever brother, especially to his jilted daughter, Catherine. *Washington Square*

ALMOND, MR. JEFFERSON: A prosperous merchant, married to Mrs. Elizabeth Almond. According to his sister-in-law he speaks indistinctly. *Washington Square*

ALMOND, MARIAN: One of the Almonds' nine children, a pretty little person of seventeen with a very small figure and a very large sash. Engaged to Arthur Townsend she already has the assurance of an established matron. Introduces Arthur's cousin Morris Townsend to her heiress cousin Catherine Sloper. *Washington Square*

ALTEMURA, CONTESSA: One of the friends of the Misses Bordereau in their period of comparative sociability. *The Aspern Papers*

AMERIGO, PRINCE: Handsome, refined but impoverished member of an old Italian family, falls in love with Charlotte Stant, but cannot marry her as she is also penniless. However, when a mutual friend, Fanny Assingham, introduces him to Charlotte's sweet, pretty, very rich friend Maggie Verver, he marries her, and rejects very honourably Charlotte's last minute hints of a future liaison. The even greater challenge of Maggie's father marrying Charlotte is at first also met with noble intentions, but eventually their partners' over-complacent neglect provokes their long-delayed love affair. However Amerigo's admiration of Charlotte is slowly eclipsed by appreciation of Maggie's concealed suspicions, enigmatic countermoves and heroic dignity; these hidden depths make him transfer his confidence to Maggie so that though he behaves as well to Charlotte as possible, her departure is a relief, and his new recognition of Maggie's qualities is his reward for his more honourable scruples. *The Golden Bowl*

AMY: A decidedly pretty girl with a nose rather too aquiline and an air of charming girlish *brusquerie*. Hearing of her fiancé Hubert Lawrence's attentions to Nora Lambert she accuses her of immodesty. However Hubert's desperately thunderous reprimand delights her, and she is reconciled to him. *Watch and Ward*

ANTIQUE DEALER, THE: The Jewish antiquary from whom Prince Amerigo and Charlotte Stant do not buy the Golden Bowl, the hidden crack in which would foreshadow or bring ill-luck on the illicit relationship that Charlotte wants but the Prince at this point rejects. Having sold it much later by a strange coincidence to the Prince's wife, Maggie Verver, the antique dealer is even more strangely conscience-stricken enough to visit her and confess the unlucky crack, and, most strangely, recognising her photographs of the Prince and Charlotte as his unsatisfied customers long ago, recounts their behaviour, thus confirming her suspicions of the now developed illicit relationship, and even more dismaying, revealing the long establishment of their intimacy. *The Golden Bowl*

ARCHER, EDITH: *see* Keyes, Mrs. Edith

ARCHER, ISABEL: A tall, slim, pretty girl of sensitivity, intelligence and courage. After a mixed, wandering education

3

(which she characteristically considers rich in opportunities rather than sordid or irregular) she is taken by her aunt Mrs. Touchett to Europe. Leaving her forceful American suitor Caspar Goodwood with some relief she refuses also to marry Lord Warburton, not loving him and still wishing to experience life freely and independently. Her cousin Ralph Touchett, loving her, as an invalid, in vain, facilitates this independence by persuading his rich, kind, dying father to leave her a fortune. Unfortunately the fortune attracts unscrupulous people, among these Mme. Merle, who plots her former lover Gilbert Osmond's marriage to Isabel. Both marry under an illusion of common interests, but these are outweighed by their different values: Isabel shares the virtues of her friends, including Ralph's generosity, Goodwood's honesty and Henrietta Stackpole's independent simplicity, and despises Gilbert's worship of noble appearances. Finally learning that Pansy, supposedly the child of Gilbert's first marriage, is really his daughter by Mme. Merle, Isabel leaves him, going to Ralph's deathbed to confess her disillusionment, but the passionate Goodwood frightens her back to the moral independence of her marital conflict. Accusing herself of looking at life 'too much as a doctor's prescription' her ambitions both lead her materially astray but prevent her essential corruption. *The Portrait of a Lady*

ARCHER, LILIAN: *see* Ludlow, Mrs. Lilian

ARCHER, MR.: Isabel Archer's handsome, much-loved father, perhaps too indifferent and free with money, as he squanders and gambles away his fortune: his eclectic education of his daughters in Europe is deplored by his critics but valued highly at least by Isabel. *The Portrait of a Lady*

ARCHER, OLD MRS.: Isabel Archer's gentle, largely hospitable grandmother, owner of the house in Albany of which Isabel retains peach-flavoured memories of happy childhood visits and which passes into her father's hands, later being sold for his daughters' benefit after his death. Here Isabel first meets Mrs. Touchett. *The Portrait of a Lady*

ARMIGER, ROSE: A young woman whose strangely light grey eyes make her seem awfully plain till the smile of her wide, full-lipped mouth makes her seem strikingly handsome. A schoolgirl friend and connection of Mrs. Julia Bream—they both detest Julia's stepmother who is also Rose's aunt—she is in love with Julia's husband Tony, though herself long engaged to Dennis Vidal. Her ruthlessness in jilting Dennis when Julia's death seems likely, and later in actually drowning Julia's child Effie to incriminate her rival Jean Martle make her something of a monster. Ironically she fascinates both Dennis and a rich neighbour Paul Beever, but never Tony. *The Other House*

ASH, SUSAN: Beale Farange's under housemaid, has to supervise his daughter Maisie whose governess is neglecting her and becoming her stepmother. Tires and embarrasses Maisie on their walks by hovering on street corners, but the tables are turned when she has to accompany Maisie and her stepfather Sir Claude to France: her insularity is scorned by the enthusiastic Maisie. *What Maisie Knew*

ASPERN, JEFFREY: A famous American poet, supposed the equal and contemporary of Byron and Shelley; also dies young. Has been amazingly attractive to women, and one of his surviving mistresses, Juliana Bordereau, still possesses in her old age some of his papers, greatly coveted by editors and biographers. *The Aspern Papers*

ASSINGHAM, COLONEL ROBERT (BOB): Totally unlike his wife Fanny, he does not react to the predicaments of others, classifying and counting on human infirmities without surprise or horror, but nevertheless appears quite a social creature; he can 'deal with things perfectly, for all his needs, without getting near them'. However he indulges his wife by acting as audience to her analytic monologues. *The Golden Bowl*

ASSINGHAM, MRS. FANNY: Though oriental in appearance, with rich complexion and crisp wavy black hair, Fanny is really a brisk, frank, curious American. This briskness, as well as want of children and wealth, makes her occupy herself—benevolently—with her friends: sympathising with Prince Amerigo, whose poverty prevents marriage to Charlotte Stant, she introduces him to the wealthy Ververs, effecting his marriage with sweet, gentle Maggie Verver. She then encourages Charlotte's marriage to Maggie's widowed father Adam. Appalled when this leads to Amerigo and Charlotte renewing their love affair, Fanny endlessly analyses their conduct and

5

blames herself, but urges the injured Maggie to have faith in the lovers' basic goodness—in symbol of which she deliberately shatters the Golden Bowl, evidence of their past guilty intimacy. Her faith is finally justified when Amerigo's return to Maggie and Charlotte's pride seem to promise a fresh start for all concerned. *The Golden Bowl*

ASSUNTA: Good-natured, smiling Italian maid of Christina Light. Remains with her after her marriage to Prince Casamassima and during her separation from him. When the Princess sells her grand possessions in order to 'live simply', Assunta's pleas for saving some things are given as the excuse for storing away many items. *Roderick Hudson* and *The Princess Casamassima*

ATHELING, LADY EMMELINE: *see* Bellegarde, Marquise de (Senior)

AUGUSTINE: Eugenia Münster's intelligent French maid and confidante, who does not understand why her brilliant mistress should settle in the pastoral innocence of New England. A spare, sober, sallow, middle-aged person, she is quite unlike the *soubrette* expected by the New Englanders. *The Europeans*

AZARINA: The old negress in a crimson turban employed by Eugenia Münster for her picturesque appearance, but whose character turns out to be disappointingly dry and prim. *The Europeans*

B

B——, MONSIGNOR: A high church dignitary and uncle of Prince Casamassima, whose estate he has controlled and increases during the Prince's minority: also locks him up to prevent his marriage to the beautiful but plebeian Christina Light. However after the Prince's majority his efforts are in vain. *Roderick Hudson*

BABCOCK, BENJAMIN ('DORCHESTER'): An earnest young Unitarian minister, native of Dorchester, Massachussetts, by the name of which town his fellow tourist in Europe Newman calls him, having some private joke about it. A small, spare man with a strikingly candid countenance, he has a weak digestion and carries America about with him in the form of a sack of hominy for his meals. For all Newman's fine moral values when compared with the corrupt European de Bellegardes, he has not the obsessive moral anxiety of Babcock, who considers him in fact dangerously lax and apologetically leaves him. *The American*

BABY, THE: The nickname of a young officer in the Rifles, an admirer of Selina Berrington's. *A London Life*

BAGGARS, THE: They dine with the Brookenhams. *The Awkward Age*

BALD or BOLD: Lionel Berrington's nursery governess who found him a handful. *A London Life*

BALDI, MME.: Christina Light's bonnet maker, into whose chic creations a note of commonness is creeping. *Roderick Hudson*

BANTLING, MR. BOB: An old friend of Ralph Touchett's, a sleek smiling man of forty, who defies conventionality by becoming Henrietta Stackpole's constant travelling companion. Finally they lapse from Platonic originality into conventional marriage, but this banality is tempered by their own sense of marrying very adventurously. *The Portrait of a Lady*

BAPTISTE: Subtlest of servants, perfectly arranging Chad Newsome's room to create the right atmosphere. *The Ambassadors*

BARRACE, MISS: A middle-aged Parisian, mature, meagre, erect and eminently gay, highly adorned and freely contradictious: her characteristics are a long-handled lorgnette and an amused if enigmatic attitude expressed in the exclamation 'oh, oh, oh!' Amuses herself by taking Strether's friend Waymarsh through the Parisian society which outrages his glowering simplicity. Never becomes involved. *The Ambassadors*

BASKERVILLE, OLD: An actor in the play during which Hyacinth Robinson first meets Princess Casamassima. *The Princess Casamassima*
References to him form part of Dashwood's and Miriam Rooth's talking 'shop'. *The Tragic Muse*

7

BAXTER: A friend who meets Roderick Hudson in Switzerland and tempts him to the gambling and social excitements of Baden, thus confirming his tendency to neglect his artistic calling. *Roderick Hudson*

BAYSWATER, DUCHESS OF: A large lady with a fine fresh colour, who is very anxious that her son Lambeth should not be 'caught' by a social climbing American. Suspecting that Bessie Alden is such a person she tries to frighten her off: Bessie's sister regrets that their abrupt departure for the continent will make the Duchess believe she has succeeded. *An International Episode*

BAYSWATER, DUKE OF: His imaginary illness is invented by his wife as an excuse to summon their son Lord Lambeth away from a dangerous flirtation in America. *An International Episode*

BEALE, MRS. (MISS OVERMORE): One of eight poor but genteel Overmore sisters, she is employed as governess by Ida Farange for little Maisie, but, having met Ida's ex-husband Beale Farange by chance, she follows Maisie against orders on her six-mouth sojourn at Beale's house, pleading devotion to her pupil. There she neglects Maisie but not her own opportunities and becomes Beale's wife. Beautiful and kind, if self-interested, she next attracts Sir Claude, Ida's new husband. Growing rapidly more mature, more handsome and more formidable, she dominates him so that, though he tries to escape from her with Maisie, she easily brings him back. Confident and not overscrupulous she has no misgivings about using Maisie to camouflage her early meetings with Sir Claude or her projected continental home with him. However, being also quite fond of Maisie she is shocked to find Maisie judging her—as not overscrupulous and therefore not reliable—and preferring the ugly, unqualified but safe governess Mrs. Wix. A survivor, Mrs. Beale has a firm grasp on Sir Claude and unlike him does not recognise any higher moral standards than her own. *What Maisie Knew*

BEAUMONT, PERCY: A barrister cousin of Lord Lambeth whom he accompanies to America and warns against Bessie Alden, wrongly suspecting her of wanting to 'catch' Lambeth. *An International Episode*

BEEVER, MR.: His half control of the Wilverley Bank is bequeathed after his death to his son Paul, his widow also having some influence. *The Other House*

BEEVER, MRS. KATE: Widow of the half-owner of the Wilverley Bank, a short, solid, determined lady with very black, very flat hair and small, amazingly expressive eyes—she is 'so early Victorian as to be almost prehistoric.' Her excellent plans for her son Paul's marriage to Jean Martle are thwarted by Jean's love for the other co-owner of the bank, Tony Bream. She is also thwarted by Paul's fascination with the sinister Rose Armiger who finally murders Tony's child. After this tragedy, Mrs. Beever resigns herself to the eclipse of her own wishes. *The Other House*

BEEVER, PAUL: Inherits from his father a half control of the Wilverley Bank. A tall fat young man with small eyes, he promises to become massive in later life, but is neither gross nor lazy. His silence is enigmatic and even his mother is uncertain whether he is stupid or clever. Persists in proposing marriage to Jean Martle because it is expected, although secretly fascinated by Rose Armiger. Fortunately refused by Jean, even in the horror of learning that Rose has murdered the little daughter of his partner Tony Bream he still offers to take her away—but again fortunately is prevented. *The Other House*

BELLEGARDE, BLANCHE DE: Daughter of Marquis Urbain. Her aunt Claire de Cintré shows her love for children by telling her a story. *The American*

BELLEGARDE, CLAIRE DE: *see* Cintré, Mme. Claire de

BELLEGARDE, MARQUIS DE (SENIOR): Father of the present Marquis, a man of high bold spirit who gives his wife cause for jealousy: however it is his refusal to marry his daughter Claire to a rich but unpleasant aristocrat that infuriates his ambitious wife, so that she turns his recovery from a fever into a relapse, and by threats and withdrawing medicine literally frightens him to death. His written deathbed accusation, kept by the servant Mrs. Bread, comes as a weapon into the hands of Newman, later injured by the Marquis' wife. *The American*

BELLEGARDE, MARQUIS DE (JUNIOR, HENRI-URBAIN): With a long lean face, high bridged nose and small opaque eyes, he is as

9

cold as his mother but less intelligent and more wooden—his high-bred courtesy is marred by misunderstandings of those outside his own circle. Opposing the American Newman's marriage to his sister Claire de Cintré, he withdraws the family's consent in a sophistical quibble upon words, and is affected only by the threat of a scandal. *The American*

BELLEGARDE, MARQUISE DE (SENIOR): A small, formidable, inscrutable old woman, with delicate face, cold blue eyes and a remarkably small mouth. Born Lady Emmeline Atheling, daughter of the English Lord St. Dunstans. The world of society, its values and taboos are sacred to her, and other values, religious or humanitarian, mean nothing to her. Thus she marries her daughter Claire to a rich, ugly old aristocrat and effects the death of her husband when he objects to this, but cannot finally agree to the widowed Claire's remarriage to a handsome, rich but plebeian American, Newman. And Newman's threat to publicise her part in her husband's death to society weighs more with her than reproaches or the loss of her daughter to a closed convent. *The American*

BELLEGARDE, MARQUISE DE (JUNIOR): The 'little marquise'—a small, pretty, restless, flighty woman of distinguished ancestry who finds married life with the stick-like Marquis a severe trial. Loves gaiety, sympathises with her sister-in-law Claire de Cintré, but plans to attend a Bohemian Ball just after Claire enters a convent. *The American*

BELLEGARDE, COMTE VALENTIN DE: Claire de Cintré's younger brother, a handsome young man of medium height and a robustness that he fears may become stoutness. His mobile face indicates the sincerity of his every mood—unlike his cold aristocratic mother and elder brother. Also unlike them he likes and befriends the American Newman, approving his engagement to Claire. Unfortunately he still subscribes to the aristocratic custom of duelling and insists on challenging Stanislas Kapp over the coquette Noémie Nioche. Fatally wounded, he is horrified to hear on his deathbed of his family's interference with Claire's engagement. Apologising for their betrayal he directs Newman to question the servant Mrs. Bread about his family's secret crime, urging him to publish it in revenge. His charm and spirit show the best of the aristocratic tradition, but Newman ultimately rejects not only the emptiness of its customs but even the idea of revenge. *The American*

BELLEVUE, LADY BEATRICE: Known in London for being 'very fast' and as such is pointed out as an interesting sight to Mrs. Westgate and Bessie Alden. *An International Episode*

BELTRAM, DR.: Aggie's and the Duchess's spiritual adviser. *The Awkward Age*

BERRINGTON, FERDY AND GEORDIE (PARSON and SCRATCH): The Berringtons' two little boys, just learning the alphabet. They are robust creatures and their aunt Laura Wing, slightly disconcerted by their apparent indifference to their mother's disappearance, reflects that, in spite of the upheaval and scandal of divorce, they 'will do anyway.' *A London Life*

BERRINGTON, LIONEL: A small man with a red, smooth, fat, suffused face, round watery eyes and a missing front tooth. His devotion to sport is evidently not his only indulgence, as his frivolous unfaithful wife Selina is at first able to make effective counter-accusations against his threats of divorce. However her elopement with a lover is well witnessed by his private detectives and he rejoices in the prospect of revenging himself in a long, scandalous divorce suit. He is quite unable to understand his sister-in-law Laura Wing's deep-felt moral horror of this rupture, and his intention to subpoena her is thoughtless rather than cruel. *A London Life*

BERRINGTON, MRS. SELINA: Laura Wing's very beautiful elder sister. Fair, slender and graceful, she can appear innocently lovely when she wishes, but her vociferous hostility to her husband, usual indifference to her two children and almost scandalously reckless social life have disillusioned and depressed her sister. Unscrupulous and determined to get her own way, Selina meets her husband's threats and Laura's appeals with outright lies and pretended repentance. With some cruelty she arranges her sudden elopement with Captain Crispin so as to be as publicly unpleasant as possible to Laura: though no more guilty perhaps than her selfish husband, Selina always has it in her to be nastier. *A London Life*

BERRINGTON, OLD MRS.: Mother of Lionel, who wishes he had married Laura Wing instead of her sister Selina. She has long cheeks, kind eyes, sedate satin streamers and reminds Laura, who likes her for her simplicity, of a tablet of fine white soap. *A London Life*

BESSIE: Daughter of Cecilia. (*See* Cecilia, Cousin) *Roderick Hudson*

BETTERMAN, MRS.: The member of the household who is supposed to look after Mrs. Assingham's guest, Charlotte Stant. Mrs. Assingham's search for her may be an excuse to leave Charlotte alone with the Prince. *The Golden Bowl*

BILHAM, JOHN LITTLE: Commonly known by his middle and last names (being, in fact, little). Coming from America to Paris to paint, he is inhibited by the study of great paintings and left without anything 'but his beautiful intelligence and his confirmed habit of Paris.' A friend of the greatly polished Chad Newsome, whose apartment and reputation he is caretaking when Strether arrives to take Chad back to America. Fond of Strether (who gives him his famous advice 'Live!'), Bilham lies to him like a gentleman to protect Chad's mistress Mme. de Vionnet, and he accompanies the pretty American Mamie Pocock and her party off on a European tour probably more to oblige Strether than with serious intentions. *The Ambassadors*

BILLINGHURST, MRS.: Sister of the late George Dallow, staying at Versailles to teach French to her daughters (she has 'a dozen or two') where Julia Dallow goodnaturedly visits her. *The Tragic Muse*

BIRDSEYE, MISS: A little old lady of about eighty with an enormous head, a vast, fair, candid brow, a pair of weak, kind, tired-looking eyes, and a countenance blurred and smoothed by the waves of sympathy of her long, philanthropic life. Her humanitarian zeal is universal and undiscriminating, but for all her confused discursiveness she has worked and suffered heroically, particularly for slave emancipation and education. At her house Verena Tarrant first meets both Olive Chancellor and Basil Ransom: Miss Birdseye's peaceful death fortunately precedes Verena's desertion of Olive and a public career for Basil and private life. *The Bostonians*

BLACKBOROUGH, MARQUIS OF: Wears a white coat and has a lisp. On the strength of his title and a speech in the House of

Lords is pointed out as an interesting sight to Mrs. Westgate and Bessie Alden. *An International Episode*

BLANCHARD, MISS AUGUSTA: A young, pretty American artist with a small income who sells her pictures in Rome; flowers painted with remarkable if finical skill are her speciality. Slender, pale and elegant, she nevertheless cannot rival Mary Garland in Rowland Mallet's memory, and eventually marries a rich, sententious widower, Mr. Leavenworth. *Roderick Hudson*

BLINT, MR.: Lady Castledean's current favourite, a sleek, civil, accomplished young man, distinctly younger than her ladyship: to camouflage his staying with her, she invites her guests Prince Amerigo and Charlotte Verver (née Stant) to stay on also. *The Golden Bowl*

BOGLE, MISS: The high attendant of the Principino in London, carries her head most aloft. *The Golden Bowl*

BOMBICCI, CAVALIERE: One of the friends of the Misses Bordereau in their period of comparative sociability. *The Aspern Papers*

BOOKER, MR.: Of Baltimore. A nice young American, invited to share an opera box with his friend Mr. Wendover and the sisters Laura Wing and Mrs. Selina Berrington. Selina's malicious demand that he does not return to chaperone the modest Laura and her escort is her parting injury as she leaves in mid-performance for her cleverly planned elopement with Crispin: Mr. Booker remains innocently bewildered by all the manoeuvring and emotion of the evening. *A London Life*

BORDEREAU, MISS JULIANA: A very old lady, survivor of an earlier era when she was mistress of a celebrated Romantic poet, Jeffrey Aspern. Now lives in poverty in Venice with her niece Tina. When the Narrator, not believing her denials that she has any of Aspern's papers, poses as a tourist and seeks lodgings with her, she agrees, though suspecting his motives, because she wishes to leave Tina more money. Her dangerous illness tempts the Narrator to see if letters are visible in her desk, but she rises, interrupts his search and collapses with the shock. This precipitates her death some days later. Very frail, small and shrunken, she always wears a large eye shade or veil but during the fatal confrontation the intruding Narrator sees that her accusing eyes are still as wonderfully beautiful as Aspern has described. *The Aspern Papers*

BORDEREAU, MISS TINA: Niece of Juliana Bordereau, she is a simple, dim, middle-aged spinster, who in contrast with her old but strong-willed aunt is 'the more deeply futile because her inefficiency was inward.' Falls in love with the Narrator whose motive in cultivating them is to obtain her aunt's letters from the dead poet Aspern. She does not condemn this motive, nor even his over-zealous prying that leads to Juliana's fury, collapse and death, but is then torn between his demands and her dead aunt's solemn last request. Summons courage to hint that he could gain a just claim on the papers by marrying her, but seeing she is quite unacceptable to him, she meekly burns the papers as Juliana directed, without bearing any resentment. *The Aspern Papers*

BOTTOMLEY, LORD: Invited to dinner at Mr. Carteret's while Nicholas Dormer is staying there. *The Tragic Muse*

BOWERBANK, MRS.: Turnkey at a women's prison where she is instrumental in bringing ten-year-old Hyacinth Robinson to his imprisoned mother's deathbed. A high-shouldered, towering majestic woman, mother of seven. *The Princess Casamassima*

BRADEEN, LADY: Her name may be Mary or Cissy, according to her frequent telegrams. Interest in her striking beauty first leads the Telegraphist to identify her correspondent and lover, the even more frequent telegrapher, Everard. After a scandal is narrowly averted, her husband unexpectedly dies and she compels Everard to marry her, though his ardour is apparently cooling. *In the Cage*

BRADY, DR.: The sweetest of little country doctors, attends the Principino whose mother the Princess (Maggie Verver) relies on his frequent visits and long discussions of what answers with his little five at home. *The Golden Bowl*

BRAND, MR.: A tall, fair, striking young man whose nose is too large and whose mouth and eyes are too small, but the expression of his little clean coloured blue eyes is irresistibly gentle and serious: he looks 'as good as gold'. A Unitarian minister, he loves Gertrude Wentworth and hopes to cure her of her 'wicked' restlessness and temper. However his attentions are irksome to her, and when she prefers her change-loving cousin Felix Young, Brand is for a time very unhappy. Encouraged then by hints that Gertrude's sister Charlotte loves him, he heroically performs Felix and Gertrude's marriage ceremony and later marries the modest, flawless Charlotte himself. *The Europeans*

BREAD, MRS. CATHERINE: A very respectable English servant, enters the de Bellegarde household when her mistress marries the Marquis, nurses Claire and Valentin de Bellegarde but, though kept on in her superseded old age, bears the Marquise a grudge for once insulting her respectability. Suspects foul play in the Marquis' last illness, receives his secret written accusation of his wife, keeps it and long afterwards gives it to the American Newman, whose marriage to her beloved Claire the other de Bellegardes have prevented. Newman pensions her in the nominal position of his Parisian housekeeper. *The American*

BREAM, EFFIE: Child of Tony Bream. Because of her dying mother's demand that she shall never have a stepmother, she is a barrier to Tony's remarriage, and is murdered on her birthday by the desperate Rose Armiger. A sweet, perfect little girl, she is simply the victim of adult passions. *The Other House*

BREAM, MRS. JULIA: Tony Bream's wife, convinced that she is dying in childbed, demands his vow never to remarry while their child lives. Ironically the vow becomes a threat not to the child's happiness but its very life. *The Other House*

BREAM, MR. PAUL: Late partner with Mr. Beever in the Wilverley Bank, leaves his share to his son Tony. *The Other House*

BREAM, TONY (ANTHONY): Co-owner of the Wilverley Bank, six years older than his partner Paul Beever. A 'very handsome, happy clever active ambitiously local young man' who quite unconsciously is 'so exaggerated'—his dress just too fine, his voice just too loud. Also unconsciously makes people like him, with fatal results, for there are rivals—Rose Armiger and Jean Martle—for his affection, though he has promised his dying wife not to marry while their daughter Effie lives.

Eventually Rose, in desperate jealousy, drowns little Effie, mainly to incriminate Jean. Horrified and shocked, he accuses himself, to protect the women involved, though finally the death is passed off as an accident. Energetic and resilient, he will probably recover and marry Jean sooner than he thinks. *The Other House*

BRÉCOURT, M. DE (ALPHONSE): Marries Susan Probert. *The Reverberator*

BRÉCOURT, MME. DE (SUSAN, SUZANNE): Daughter of Mr. Probert, has a fine plain face, flaxen hair, vivid red lips, and protuberant light eyes. Favourite sister of Gaston, the most modern, Parisian and inflammable member of the family, with imagination, humour, generosity, enthusiasm and even infatuation. Thus she is Gaston's spokesman and advocate in persuading their family to accept his fiancée Francie Dosson: she also continues longest to suggest excuses when Francie innocently passes on for publication scandal about the family. *The Reverberator*

BRIDGET, LADY: Mother of Lord Deepmere and only child of Lord Finucane from whom she has inherited 'no end of things'. *The American*

BRIGSTOCK, MRS. ADELA: Mona's mother, a foolish and taste-less woman, with a face of which it is 'impossible to say anything but that it was pink,' and a mind to match which 'strayed and bleated like an unbranded sheep.' *The Spoils of Poynton*

BRIGSTOCK, MONA: A straight, fair young lady, her pretty face completely devoid of expression and her mind devoid of taste. Becoming engaged to Owen Gereth she is quite un-appreciative of his inherited home Poynton and its priceless treasures. However, from possessiveness and self-assertion she determines to be mistress of all the treasures when Owen's mother, whose hostility she resents, illegally spirits many of them away. Her making their restitution a condition of their marriage repels Owen and throws him into the arms of the more delicate Fleda Vetch, but Mona, possessiveness roused again, and learning of the premature return of the treasures, somehow ensnares Owen into having to marry her quickly and privately after all. Her ruthlessness is a strength derived from her insensitivity, but once victorious her natural, even good humour and charm seem to reassert themselves and keep Owen subjected. *The Spoils of Poynton*

BRINDER, SIR JOHN: Attends a great ball with the Ambassador's party, and rather artlessly attaches himself to the beautiful Mrs. Verver (Charlotte Stant). Fanny Assingham competently detaches him. *The Golden Bowl*

BRISSENDEN, MRS. GRACE: A woman who, from being notoriously older than Guy when she marries him, and moreover rather plain, becomes progressively younger and prettier-looking, seeming to draw these qualities from her husband who meanwhile is becoming amazingly aged. She then apparently is involved in a love affair with Gilbert Long, similarly a beneficiary of a transfusion of new wit and perception from a mistress, probably May Server. At the Newmarch house party Mrs. Brissenden tries to mislead the Narrator, whose interest in all these relationships threatens her secret, by suggesting various sources for Long's allegiance, but finally ventures the bold fiction that Long is the lover of clever Lady John and really no cleverer himself than before. *The Sacred Fount*

BRISSENDEN, GUY: Originally a handsome young man of about thirty who during five or six years of marriage to a woman ten years older than himself somehow transfers his youth and beauty to her, becoming terribly aged as she grows younger. Apparently unaware of this, he nevertheless mopes miserably and falls back on dumb resigned comradeship with May Server, victim of a similar sacrifice of her wit and perception to her once dull lover Long: meanwhile their partners, Mrs. Brissenden and Long, are pairing off and neglecting them. *The Sacred Fount*

BRIVES, MME. DE: Among the guests of Mme. de Brécourt whose brother Gaston Probert prefers to dine with the newly met Dossons. No longer young but very attractive she flirts with the Proberts' brother-in-law Maxime de Cliché. *The Reverberator*

BRODERIP, MR.: An old gentleman of Salem who was Mr. Wentworth's classmate at Harvard in 1809 and is still his friend. *The Europeans*

BROOKENHAM, EDWARD: Nanda's father, a lean, bony man with a pale cold face and hard handsome features, but somehow no accent or significance in appearance or manner. Has an ugly little property in Gloucestershire which is usually rented out to increase his income. Is generally held to be extremely adequate and efficient in action, in spite of his unresponsive dryness—he has a professional position in Rivers and Lakes—but is of no importance in his family. *The Awkward Age*

BROOKENHAM, MRS. FERNANDA (MRS. BROOK): Though in her forty-first year and mother of four children she is still charmingly pretty—she has and will always have 'the pure light of youth'. However she prevents her eighteen-year-old daughter Nanda from joining her drawing-room society less from the reflection on her own age than from fear of constraint, her society depending on frank, witty and scandalous discussion of its members and friends. Her dominance here derives from both her characteristic feather-headed wit and her genuine interest in personal problems. Treating her daughter as a friend instead of with parental responsibility, she is to blame for Nanda's not marrying, first through bundling her off unsupervised to mix with unsuitable friends, and then through influencing Vanderbank against marrying her, as she wants him herself. His embarrassment after this, and another friend, Mitchett, marrying not happily, break up her circle of cronies, and she remains solitary until Nanda, the more motherly of the two, about to leave home herself, urges everyone to return to her unfailingly young and attractive mother. *The Awkward Age*

BROOKENHAM, HAROLD: Eldest of the Brookenham children, a small slightly stooping young man of insidiously acute appearance—he has the voice of a man of forty, and he dresses to match. His family's lack of responsibility to him is financial and he ekes out a living by inhabiting other people's country houses and borrowing five-pound notes. *The Awkward Age*

BROOKENHAM, NANDA: A girl of eighteen, with the delicate, old-fashioned beauty of her grandmother Lady Julia, which endears her to Lady Julia's rich old former suitor Mr. Longdon, though he is shocked to find her own character is incongruously that of a modern, emancipated girl. Nanda has considerable knowledge of the world and human nature,

18

her innocence consisting of her matter-of-fact attitude to this knowledge, unlike the guilty enjoyment of scandal common in her mother's salon: ironically to keep her from this salon she has been sent to mix with an even more disreputable circle of friends. Unfortunately Vanderbank whom she loves does not love her and is shocked at her awareness of the matters he gossips about, and Mr. Longdon's bribe of a dowry is foiled by Mrs. Brookenham's influence—she also loves him and wants to keep him to herself. Unable to reject her own modernity, and unable to reproach her mother, whose problems are also real, Nanda accepts her situation and Mr. Longdon's offer of a home. *The Awkward Age*

BROOKSES, MR. and SNOOKSES, MR.: Imaginary typical guests to be 'received' by Mamie Pocock. *The Ambassadors*

BROWN, LUCINDA: An elderly woman of exemplary virtue, formerly maid to Roger Lawrence's mother, now his housekeeper. On reflection welcomes his adoption of Nora Lambert as likely to increase rather than diminish her sphere of authority, and, spinster as she is, assumes vast feminine wisdom in discussing Nora's upbringing. *Watch and Ward*

BUBB, MRS.: One of the clients for whom Mrs. Jordan does the flower arrangements. *In the Cage*

BUCKTON, MR.: The Telegraphist's fellow worker at Mr. Cocker's general Post Office, and her enemy: there is rivalry between them for the most interesting customers. *In the Cage*

BUFFERY, MR.: The doctor from round the corner who attends Miss Pynsent in her last illness. He does not have a very large practice, but is apparently really clever. *The Princess Casamassima*

BURFIELD'S: A name in the code used by Everard and Lady Bradeen to conceal their intrigue. *In the Cage*

BURRAGE, MR. HENRY: A rather handsome, rich, dilettante law student at Harvard, a precocious good-natured man of the world. Falls in love with Verena Tarrant, and would seem in his niceness, culture, and willingness to encourage her public speaking career, to be a serious temptation to Verena's dedication to women's emancipation. However her greater attraction to the proud, poor and reactionary Basil Ransom means that Burrage's virtues are of no avail. *The Bostonians*

BURRAGE, MRS.: Mother of Henry Burrage and an important society hostess in New York, 'slightly irritable with cleverness and at the same time good natured with prosperity.' At first opposes her son's love for the public speaker Verena Tarrant, but later is won round to encourage it—in vain, for Verena rejects him. *The Bostonians*

BUTTERWORTHS, MR. AND MRS.: Entertain the Duke of Green-Erin hospitably, but when they call on him in England he insultingly supposes their only motive is to regain an unpaid debt. (A warning tale told by Mrs. Westgate.) *An International Episode*

BUTTRICK, DR.: Sir Luke Strett reminds Mrs. Stringham of this great man. *The Wings of the Dove*

C

CALDERONI: Prince Amerigo's man of business, fresh from Rome to arrange his client's marriage settlements, and is 'shown' London by the Prince's courteous future father-in-law, millionaire Adam Verver. *The Golden Bowl*

CAPTAIN, THE: A fair, sunburnt man with simple, kind, light blue eyes. Admires Ida Farange whole-heartedly, considering her an angel, good and true. This reduces her little daughter Maisie to tears, being the only kind words she has ever heard of her mother. However he evidently is disillusioned for Ida later calls him 'the biggest cad in London'. *What Maisie Knew*

CARDINAL, THE: Prince Amerigo's great-uncle, who has taken a hand in his nephew's education and has a strong character. *The Golden Bowl*

CARRÉ, MME. HONORINE: An ageing, great French actress whose first comment on Miriam Rooth is unfavourable, but after being badgered and intrigued by Miriam's persistence and dedication agrees to teach her and admits her latent genius. Superficially a red-faced woman in a wig, her whole appearance is in fact an infinitely delicate and variable instrument. Her own commitment to Art above all prudent, social and conventional values is a lesson both to Miriam and to Nick Dormer. *The Tragic Muse*

CARTERET, MR. CHARLES: Old friend of the late Sir Nicholas Dormer whose views and pure, anxious, benevolent character he shares. Later assists his friend's son Nick with sums of money and pages of political advice. Nearly eighty and increasingly frail, though still shy and childlike, he promises a large legacy to Nick as well as a settlement on his marriage to Julia Dallow. But when Nick is jilted by Julia and, instead of protesting, abandons politics for art, Mr. Carteret disinherits him. Though gentle and innocent he has a rather deadly impassivity towards anything outside his understanding. *The Tragic Muse*

CASAMASSIMA, PRINCE: Last of an ancient line of Neapolitan princes, whose inheritance has been nursed during his minority. He is ugly, though distinguished looking, with a dull eye and refined features. The Prince wishes to marry the beautiful Christina Light, submitting to her caprices and indifference with bewilderment, being proud and conscious of his own worth. In spite of his general amiability he has temper, bigotry and 'an immense heritage of more or less aggressive traditions' that make him formidable when Christina finally marries him. During their marriage jealousy is added to his wounded pride, and after throwing her out of his house (after great provocation) he has to appeal in vain for her forgiveness. His shocked reactions lend spice to her involvement in revolutionary movements, and by the time he brings himself to interview her friend Hyacinth Robinson, he is almost distracted. Eventually he withdraws the Princess's allowance, and Paul Muniment predicts that she will have to return to him. *Roderick Hudson* and *The Princess Casamassima*

CASAMASSIMA, PRINCESS: Née Christina Light. After ten years of marriage she retains her perfect dazzling beauty, but having quarrelled with her husband, put him in the wrong and left him, she is still searching for some interest or motive in life. Daring, original and superbly unconventional as ever, she combines charitable interest in the poor with revolutionary plotting for their benefit, and therefore gets to know Hyacinth Robinson, attached to the fringe of a revolutionary group. Her real affection for his sweet, romantic, unusual character is eclipsed by the excitement of dangerous politics and by his more impressive friend Paul Muniment, just as, ironically, Hyacinth has become reconciled to the world of culture and privilege by her influence. Though her own commitment seems mainly sincere there is also an element of histrionics in her fervour. Characteristically, having driven Hyacinth by her neglect to suicide, she alone perceives his intention—though she arrives too late to save him. When her outraged husband finally stops her income, Paul predicts that she will return to the matrimonial fold, but her complex and unpredictable character leaves her future uncertain. *See also* Light, Christina. *The Princess Casamassima*

CASHMORE, LADY FANNY: Lord Petherton's magnificent, simple, stupid sister, whose black hair, heavy blue eyes and low forehead just miss seeming dangerously sultry. Her affairs are among the chief interests of Mrs. Brookenham's salon—where her friends are always persuading her not to elope with a lover. Her annoyance at her husband's rumoured affair with Carrie Donner is tempered by satisfaction at his equal culpability. *The Awkward Age*

CASHMORE, MR.: Rich, large, jaunty and massive without majesty, he would be very red-haired if he were not very bald. His exasperation with his flighty, extravagant wife Lady Fanny is less righteous because of his suspected affair with Carrie Donner, but this is either prevented or stopped by Nanda Brookenham's good influence (and counter-attractions). *The Awkward Age*

CASTLEDEAN, LADY: Not wishing for propriety's sake to remain conspicuously alone with her young man Mr. Blint, she asks two more of her guests, Prince Amerigo and Charlotte Stant, to remain rather longer at her country house—this then provides the latter two with the opportunity of beginning their love affair. The Prince's wife (Maggie Verver) is interested in Lady Castledean without really liking her though she has the biggest diamonds, the yellowest hair, the longest lashes on the falsest eyes, the rightest manner on the wrongest assumption (i.e. that she always keeps every advantage). Her kind of social and personal double dealing is an element Maggie has to recognise and come to terms with. *The Golden Bowl*

CASTLEDEAN, LORD: Lady Castledean's husband but, so very oddly, given the personage and the type, a rather large item in the social system. Therefore he has to go up to London during the week leaving his wife free in their country house. *The Golden Bowl*

CATCHING, MISS: A young lady with fair ringlets and refined anxious expression, who works on the Harvard library catalogue. A friend of Verena Tarrant, she shows round Verena and Basil Ransom, to whom she seems a typical New England girl. *The Bostonians*

CATHERINE, MOTHER: An elderly French nun of fresh complexion, full cheeks and with spectacles. Takes charge of Pansy Osmond in her convent education and escorts her home. *The Portrait of a Lady*

CAVALIERE, THE: *see* Giacosa, The Cavaliere Giuseppe

CECILIA, COUSIN: The clever, pretty, lively, 28-year-old widow of Rowland Mallet's cousin. Left with little money she educates her little girl Bessie admirably and skilfully conceals her poverty so that she and her home are always elegant and cheerful. She cultivates the young would-be sculptor Roderick Hudson not to benefit him but to alleviate her own boredom, and displays characteristic sharp sarcasm when Rowland, to whom she has introduced him, takes him away to Rome. Rowland corresponds with her about Roderick's rise, decline and fall over the next two years. *Roderick Hudson*

CHANCELLOR, OLIVE: A young woman of Boston, pale, thin, green-eyed, with a character of almost tragic intensity. Though intolerant of all social abuses, her attraction to the young, bright, gifted women's rights speaker Verena Tarrant involves her particularly in the women's emancipation campaign. Being, unlike Verena, 'all of a piece' Olive consecrates her own and Verena's life totally to the cause, buying off Verena's family and suffering anxiety over the counterclaims of her many suitors. Ironically it is Olive's own reactionary Mississipian cousin Basil Ransom who, being very hostile to her beliefs, carries off Verena at the very opening of her greatest public meeting, leaving Olive alone to face the disappointed audience. Though lacking in humour and sense of proportion, Olive is intelligent as well as sensitive, but this morbid sensitivity turns her sense of duty into a torment. *The Bostonians*

CHATTERTON, MRS.: A New York lady, a great talker who reports Hubert Lawrence's engagement to a certain rich young lady. *Watch and Ward*

CHAYTER: Mr. Carteret's 'immemorial blank butler', so like his master they might have been twins if he permitted his face any expression. Takes it on himself to send for Nicholas Dormer at Mr. Carteret's last illness, and receives a large legacy though Nicholas is disinherited. *The Tragic Muse*

CHIPPERFIELD, MRS.: Sister of Mrs. Bowerbank and mother of nine children. Her dropsical husband is an undertaker, which business is 'a blessing because you could always count on it.' *The Princess Casamassima*

CHURTONS, THE: Some of the English friends who visit the Misses Bordereau in their period of comparative sociability. *The Aspern Papers*

CINTRÉ, MME. CLAIRE DE: Née de Bellegarde. A cool, fair, very gentle woman, married to her horror to the ugly, unpleasant, painted Comte de Cintré. After being widowed she lives again quite under the authority of her mother and elder brother, partly through her timidity, partly through inculcated filial piety, partly as an agreed reparation for renouncing some of the count's ill-gotten property. When they reluctantly agree that the rich but plebeian American Newman may at least court her she is soon won by his warmth and generosity, but when her family abandons neutrality and forbids their marriage she feels unable to defy them. However she escapes further coercion by entering a closed Carmelite convent. Her strength is for endurance, not action. *The American*

CINTRÉ, M. DE: A 55-year-old aristocrat, ugly, rich, five feet high and paints his face. His recommendation as suitor for Claire de Bellegarde is indifference to her small dowry. He dies, disappointing her family by having already spent his fortune, and disappointing his own family by having misappropriated funds held in trust for them—Claire recompenses them from her own legacy. *The American*

CLARISSE, MLLE.: Young Mme. de Bellegarde's maid: an insult about Mrs. Bread made to her, and repeated, causes resentment with important results. *The American*

CLAUDE, SIR: A very handsome, fair, polished gentleman, who marries the older, divorced Ida Farange, and takes an interest in her daughter Maisie—proclaiming himself a family man *manqué*—and perhaps his reproaches on her neglect of Maisie contribute to the quarrels that eventually alienate them. Through Maisie he meets her father's second wife Mrs. Beale, and although he will not involve Maisie in arranging clandestine meetings as Mrs. Beale hopes, being more scrupulous than she, he shows his weakness in trying to hide and evade the problems of their relationships. He tries to escape the threat of Mrs. Beale's dominance by fleeing with Maisie to Boulogne, but, once freed from obvious restraints by Ida's formal desertion of him, he returns at Mrs. Beale's summons, to the exasperation of Maisie's governess Mrs. Wix. Now repressing his scruples, he suggests that Maisie live with him and Mrs. Beale on the Continent to provide respectability, and when Maisie challenges him to leave the dangerous dominance of Mrs. Beale, he cannot, and, understanding her misgivings, lets her go with Mrs. Wix. His greater awareness of moral standards is useless as he is too weak to stand by them. *What Maisie Knew*

CLICHÉ, M. DE (MAXIME): Marries Margaret Probert and turns out not quite the pearl he was thought, though Margaret's long lugubrious face may be partly responsible for his flirtations, which are among the distressing scandals published in the *Reverberator*. *The Reverberator*

CLICHÉ, MME. DE (MARGARET, MARGUERITE, MARGOT): Gaston Probert's tall, long-faced, proud sister, least liked by his fiancée Francie Dosson, whom Mme. de Cliché unfortunately sees walking alone with Mr. Flack, who later publishes Francie's innocent gossip about the Proberts in the *Reverberator*. *The Reverberator*

CLICHÉ, OLD MME. DE: Reported to have had a horrid reputation: this objection to her son's marriage to Margaret Probert is unwisely overlooked. *The Reverberator*

CLIMBER, MISS: Of Wilmington, Delaware; she travels on the Continent and meets her friend Henrietta Stackpole by chance in London. *The Portrait of a Lady*

CLIMBER, ANNIE: 'Poor, plain little Annie', while travelling with her sister in Italy, receives three offers of marriage, which illustrates for her suspicious friend Henrietta Stackpole the dangers of the Continent. *The Portrait of a Lady*

COCKER, MR.: Owner of Cocker's, the general Post Office in Mayfair where the Telegraphist works. *In the Cage*

COLLINGWOODS, THE: Acquaintances of Selina Berrington: being (unlike the Berringtons) a happy pair they need make no secret of going to different parties after dining out, and the good Mrs. Collingwood's acceptance of a lift from Selina, implying a rather ignoble tolerance of Selina's shady reputation, bewilders the inexperienced Laura Wing. *A London Life*

CONDRIP, MR.: Parson of a dull suburban parish, with a saintly profile kept always in evidence. Marries Marian Croy whose rich aunt is disgusted with his fatuous behaviour and disowns her. He dies young, leaving his impoverished widow with four small children. *The Wings of the Dove*

CONDRIP, MRS. MARIAN: Formerly a mild sister to Kate, she becomes querulous, red and almost fat after marriage and widowhood. She considers that Kate has an obligation to submit to their rich aunt and pass along any benefits received to the Condrips. *The Wings of the Dove*

CONDRIPS, THE LITTLE: Marian's four children, Bertie, Maudie, Kitty and Guy. *The Wings of the Dove*

CONDRIPS, THE MISSES: Sisters of the late Mr. Condrip, who visit his widow too often, long and voraciously for her sister Kate Croy's liking, and discuss Kate's affairs. Without loving them Mrs. Condrip defends them touchily for their nearness to her husband. *The Wings of the Dove*

COOPER'S: A name in the code used by Everard and Lady Bradeen to conceal their intrigue. *In the Cage*

COSTELLO, MRS.: Winterbourne's aunt, a widow with a great deal of striking white hair, a fortune, much distinction and regular sick-headaches. Her society in New York is as exclusive as that of Europe where she is travelling: by the standards of both she condemns the tourist Daisy Miller as common and vulgar. *Daisy Miller*

COUNT, THE: One of Ida Farange's admirers, only five feet high and red as a lobster. *What Maisie Knew*

COUNTESS, THE: A short, fat, whiskered, wheedling woman, with overlarge nose, too small eyes and a very brown complexion. Her title is 'an American one' and she is very rich, which is why Beale Farange is her lover. Her appearance, in spite of an evident desire to be kind, irrationally repels Maisie, Beale's daughter, and makes her reverse her unwelcome decision to accompany them to America. *What Maisie Knew*

COURAGEAU, M. DE: Among the guests of Mme. de Brécourt whose brother Gaston Probert prefers to dine with the newly-met Dossons. *The Reverberator*

CRICHTON, MR.: Custodian of one of the richest departments of the British Museum, the most accomplished and obliging of public functionaries: his advice aids Mr. Verver's collecting. Invites Maggie Verver in to examine the Museum's archives on the family of her husband Prince Amerigo. *The Golden Bowl*

CRISPIN, CAPTAIN CHARLEY: A tall gentleman with a tawny beard, his most noted feature; Selina Berrington's lover, with whom she eventually elopes. *A London Life*

CROOKENDEN, THE MISSES: The half a dozen daughters of Mr. Crookenden, all with large faces and short legs, who play the piano without talent. *The Princess Casamassima*

CROOKENDEN, MR. (OLD CROOK): A prince of bookbinders, employing several men in his Soho workshops, among them Poupin, at whose request he takes on Hyacinth Robinson as an apprentice. A working craftsman who wears an apron rather dirtier than the rest, he nevertheless lives in a villa all but detached out at Putney. *The Princess Casamassima*

CROOKENDEN, MRS.: Has aspirations to gentility and gives musical evenings dressed in a headdress of cockatoo feathers and glass beads. *The Princess Casamassima*

CROTTY, SUSAN: A poor protegée of the Princess Casamassima and Lady Aurora Langrish. Her husband's ticket-of-leave (from gaol) is a common subject of interest for them. *The Princess Casamassima*

CROUCHER, MRS.: Lives on Fifty-sixth Street in New York. At the centre of a circle of women's rights sympathisers visited by Olive Chancellor and Verena Tarrant. *The Bostonians*

CROY, KATE: A beautiful English girl, slender, graceful and fine with dark hair, dark blue eyes and a character strong enough for heroic deeds, though perhaps therefore lacking in finest delicacy. Rescued from poverty and her father's disgrace by her Aunt Maud Lowder, who plans a great match for her, Kate is secretly engaged to a poor journalist Merton Densher, but hopes Aunt Maud or some good fortune will raise him above the genteel poverty she hates. When her new, rich American friend Milly Theale falls in love with Densher, Kate and he pretend he loves Kate in vain and may turn to Milly, partly to deceive Aunt Maud, partly to help Milly in her increasingly obvious illness, and partly in hopes of Milly's money, even if Densher has to become her widower to get it. This bold, daring scheme is Kate's, and she is brave enough also to visit Densher in his rooms, his condition for complying. However Milly's generosity when, discovering the deception and dying in despair, she nevertheless leaves him a large fortune, places Kate's comparative self-interest in an unfavourable light. Refusing Densher's challenge to marry him without the money, she also refuses the money alone: she is not entirely mercenary, but has been changed by the long deception. *The Wings of the Dove*

CROY, LIONEL: Father of Kate Croy. His appearance as a perfect English gentleman 'all pink and silver as to skin and hair, all straightness as to dress', and even his 'kind safe eyes' are a hollow deception: he is a hypocritical confidence trickster, leaving his own family poor and disgraced by an unmentioned crime. Wishing to claim Kate's adoption by a rich aunt as desertion, he is disconcerted by her offer to stand by him, but typically turns it to her disadvantage, claiming she is losing the family's (i.e. his) opportunities for selfish aims. Reappears later, a broken, frightened man. *The Wings of the Dove*

CROY, MARIAN: *see* Condrip, Mrs. Marian

CROY, MRS.: Disgraced by her husband Lionel she makes brief but repeated trips to foreign towns as weak and expensive attempts at economy. Dies after a painful illness, leaving a small sum to her daughters Kate and Marian. *The Wings of the Dove*

CROYS, THE YOUNG: Kate Croy and her sister Marian survive their two brothers, one of whom dies of typhoid; the other drowns. *The Wings of the Dove*

CUDDON, MRS.: One of Beale Farange's women friends. His wife wrongly assumes the Countess is Mrs. Cuddon, seeing her with Beale. *What Maisie Knew*

CUMNOR, JOHN: The Narrator's fellow biographer and editor of the poet Jeffrey Aspern. They have pioneered and promoted revival of interest in Aspern and Cumnor's direct but snubbed approach to Miss Bordereau for her Aspern papers is continued more obliquely by the Narrator. *The Aspern Papers*

CURD, SARAH: Mrs. Brookenham's second housemaid. On her own principle that one's essential nature shows itself in how one treats one's second housemaid, Mrs. Brookenham comes out well, treating both Sarah Curd and her rather inconvenient daughter Nanda with unresentful 'niceness'. *The Awkward Age*

D

DALLOW, GEORGE: Julia Dallow's late husband. Has a kindly uniform nature but is an assiduous, discriminating collector of precious *objets d'art*, about which he likes to talk with friendly tiresome competence. He leaves Julia very rich. *The Tragic Muse*

DALLOW, MRS. JULIA: A distinguished, beautiful woman, sister of Peter Sherringham, early widowed and very ambitious for political influence and fame. In love with her second cousin Nick Dormer she helps get him elected to Parliament and agrees to marry him, but is troubled by his conflicting ambition to paint portraits (she considers this low). This and jealousy at finding him painting the actress Miriam Rooth make her jilt him. Her relenting later appears in her attentions to his family and eventually she asks indirectly to sit for her portrait. Their reconciliation seems likely. *The Tragic Muse*

DANDELARD, MME.: A little Italian woman legally separated from her rakish, brutish French husband. Very pretty and childlike, her inevitable descent into amateur prostitution is foreseen philosophically by Valentin de Bellegarde but actively deprecated by Newman. *The American*

DASHWOOD, BASIL: Stage name of Mrs. Lovick's brother Arty: a tall, fair, very handsome man whose distinction is his unmistakable appearance of a gentleman, which is unvarying on stage and off. Helps and encourages Miriam Rooth to become an actress, comes to manage all her affairs and eventually marries her—less for passion than as a convenience to her career. *The Tragic Muse*

DAVENANT, LADY: A shrewd old lady of eighty, who visits country houses and reads a great deal, drawing from both occupations a fund of interesting ideas. Though peremptory and unsentimental she takes interest in Laura Wing, advising her to feel less involved in (without condoning) her sister's flighty way of life. Gives Laura refuge after her sister's scandalous elopement, and influences her admirer Mr. Wendover to deepen his admiration into love, encouraging his courtship though annoyed by Laura's final desperate appeal to her hardened sister. Later sends her money. *A London Life*

DAVIS, DR.: The Millers' doctor in Schenectady where he 'stands at the very top'. Understands Mrs. Miller's constitution as no one else does and she greatly misses him in Europe. *Daisy Miller*

DEEPMERE, LORD: A very rich English peer, with Irish connections and estates also, cousin of the de Bellegardes. Though three or four and thirty he has a bald head and two missing front teeth, but his simplicity and frank, natural smile show his youth. His basic honesty appears in his refusing to try to detach Claire de Cintré from her fiancé Newman as her mother Mme. de Bellegarde urges him—he at once reveals this plot to Claire—but any greater delicacy is beyond him: he is later seen escorting Noémie Nioche, knowing her to have caused the duel that killed his cousin Valentin de Bellegarde. *The American*

DEEPMERE, LORD: Said by Lionel Berrington to have been his wife Selina's former lover. *A London Life*

DELAMERE, MRS.: A former ornament of the English stage (whom the great Mme. Carré has never heard of) who gives lessons to a very few—including Miriam Rooth—as a great favour and without any apparent good effect. *The Tragic Muse*

DELANCEY: Self-styled soda water manufacturer, though in appearance strangely like a hairdresser. He wishes to 'change everything' except religion of which he approves, and it is his challenge that provokes Hyacinth Robinson's offer of revolutionary action and his involvement in an assassination plot. *The Princess Casamassima*

DENCE, SIR DIGBY: Head of the General Audit office where Vanderbank works. *The Awkward Age*

DENSHER, MERTON: A longish, leanish, fairish young man, 'only half a Briton' being educated, as the son of a chaplain working abroad, mainly in Swiss schools and a German University, though followed by Cambridge. As a journalist his lack of income and pushiness means he will never be rich, especially not rich enough for his cautious, determined fiancée Kate Croy. To placate Kate's rich aunt and to help her new, rich and very ill American friend Milly Theale, Densher pretends to be unsuccessful with Kate and susceptible to Milly, Kate's plan being that Milly shall leave him money. Initially rebellious, he agrees on condition that Kate comes to him in his rooms. His indifference to Milly becomes affection, but when the truth is guessed and betrayed by his rival Lord Mark, Densher is unable to deny Kate outright—even though his denial might save Milly's will to live. However, understanding and forgiving this, Milly leaves him a fortune when she dies. At last appreciative of her, he is repelled by Kate's more self-interested courage, and challenges her to marry him without his inheritance, 'as we were'. Kate refuses both this and the money alone, and they part for ever: he has been saved from the sordid effects of the plot by his own sense of honour and Milly's example, but the result is that both have changed too much to be 'as we were'. *The Wings of the Dove*

DENSHER, MRS.: Mother of Merton Densher, wife of a British chaplain abroad, she is unconventional and talented enough to supplement his small stipend by copying old masters and selling her work to tourists. *The Wings of the Dove*

DENT-DOUGLAS, CAPTAIN: Wants to elope with Lady Fanny Cashmore. *The Awkward Age*

DOLMAN, MISS: Addressee of telegrams from Captain Everard and Lady Bradeen, whose intrigues involve sending her code names such as 'Burfield's' and 'Cooper's'. *In the Cage*

DONNER, MRS. CARRIE: Sister of Tishy Grendon, irregularly pretty and painfully shy, but the paint on her face is so obvious that she should 'either have left more to nature or taken more from art.' Thought to be Mr. Cashmore's mistress, though Nanda Brookenham (whose reputation suffers from knowing her at all) defends her innocence. *The Awkward Age*

DORCHESTER: *see* Babcock, Benjamin

DORMER, LADY AGNES: Widow of Sir Nicholas, a handsome woman of cold, austere, firm appearance. After her husband's early death ends his promising political career she is irked by her elder son Percy's selfish frivolity and her own reduced circumstances, and pins her hopes on her son Nick who is to follow in his father's footsteps. Encouraging him to re-enter Parliament and become engaged to the politically influential Julia Dallow, she is appalled when his disagreement with Julia is followed by his leaving politics to become an artist. Only her daughter Biddy's entry into public life by marrying diplomat Peter Sherringham somewhat consoles her. Though persistently morose, she is a 'high executive woman, the mother of children, the daughter of earls, the consort of an official, the dispenser of hospitality' and naturally the frustration of all her powers instils self-interest into her maternal ambitions. *The Tragic Muse*

DORMER, BIDDY (BRIDGET): A straight, slender, grey-eyed girl, very pretty, whose sweet nature makes her generally liked, but she loves her childhood friend Peter Sherringham without return, especially after he falls in love with actress Miriam Rooth. Her modelling in clay shows a small talent, but she is the only member of the family to sympathise with her brother Nick's renunciation of politics for art. Eventually marries Peter when he realises that Miriam is not for him. *The Tragic Muse*

DORMER, GRACE: Elder daughter of Lady Agnes, less pretty than Biddy. Rather tactless and stolid, she will probably never marry. *The Tragic Muse*

DORMER, SIR NICHOLAS: Famous as a rising politician (especially for his characteristic 'coordinating power in relation to detail') and sees his son young Nick also enter Parliament unusually early, but dies before his son loses his seat again in an unexpected election. His deathbed advice weighs heavily upon Nick who is tempted by an artistic vocation. *The Tragic Muse*

DORMER, NICK (NICHOLAS): A handsome, very English young man, upon whose successful emulation of his father's political career depend his mother's hopes, his prospective marriage to rich, ambitious Julia Dallow, and an inheritance from his father's old friend Mr. Carteret. Dutifully renouncing dreams of becoming a painter, he enters Parliament, but when Julia, distrusting his commitment and jealous of his painting actress Miriam Rooth, breaks off their engagement, Nicholas leaves politics and, Mr. Carteret thereupon disinheriting him, becomes an impoverished artist. His interest in the fascinating Miriam is however artistic, and when Julia makes a move of reconciliation he will probably be reconciled to her, though not to politics. A man of eager enthusiasm and quick intellect, he finds this quickness something of a curse, as he grasps both political issues and artistic skills too easily, without needing to acquire the real mastery necessary for great achievement; realising this, he fears easy success. *The Tragic Muse*

DORMER, SIR PERCIVAL (PERCY, Senior): Uncle of Percy and Nick, dies wifeless and childless—said to have been like his raffish nephew Percy. *The Tragic Muse*

DORMER, SIR PERCIVAL (PERCY, Junior): Does not resemble his

father Sir Nicholas, spends all his time roaming the world shooting big and small game, letting out the family home to Americans. Surprises everyone by marrying his mistress, a robust countrywoman, thus legitimising their past and future issue. *The Tragic Muse*

DOSSON, DELIA (FIDELIA): A 25-year-old American whose large white face is blank with a suggestion of obstinacy, but neither stupid nor displeasing, though not even Paris can make her thick figure look elegant. Her ambitions and plans centre mainly on her beautiful younger sister Francie, and being hostile to George Flack she influences the indifferent Francie against him, promoting instead her engagement to the more exotic Gaston Probert. Though bewildered and annoyed at his family's objections to the publicity Francie has innocently brought to their private scandals, Delia intends to make social use of the Proberts after a decent interval. *The Reverberator*

DOSSON, FRANCIE (FRANCINE): Though little more imaginative or intellectual than her sister Delia, Francie is exceedingly, extraordinarily pretty, with a kind of still radiance, and in fact has potentialities for development. Though she gossips about her fiancé Gaston Probert and his family to her rejected suitor George Flack, she has not realised how much of this he will publish in his journal the *Reverberator*, nor how much the Proberts will be distressed, and unlike Delia she comes to understand something of their foreign reticence and sensitivity to publicity. As her essential innocence is evident in this, Gaston leaves his cherished family to stand by her. *The Reverberator*

DOSSON, MR. WHITNEY: Father of Delia and Francie, a fair, spare, unobtrusive, unassertive business man who has 'a natural financial faculty of the finest order' which has made him very rich without particular will-power or ambition. Thinks more of his daughters than of anything else and spends his time in Europe placidly contemplating their activities, otherwise pleased only if he can ensure good conditions by paying heavily himself. However after the rupture with the family of Francie's fiancé Gaston Probert, he is surprisingly adamant against ever forgiving them. *The Reverberator*

DOSSON, MRS.: Now dead. Mr. Dosson's decisive courtship of her contrasts with Gaston Probert's cautious, correct, European approach to their daughter Francie. *The Reverberator*

DOUGLAS: The owner of the manuscript of the ghost story, written and given to him by its narrator, the Governess, whom he has known and greatly liked. Retells the ghost story himself at a country house party. *The Turn of the Screw*

D'OUTREVILLE, DUCHESSE: As the greatest lady in France (in more ways than one) she is presented to Newman by the de Bellegardes, at his engagement party: she reminds him of the fat lady at a fair. After being deprived of his fiancée by the de Bellegardes, Newman visits the duchesse intending to reveal an old scandal about them in revenge, but finds he does not wish to be involved in any way in the society she represents, even for revenge, and departs without speaking. *The American*

D'OUTREVILLE, MME.: Among the guests of Mme. de Brécourt, whose brother Gaston Probert prefers to dine with the newly-met Dossons. She calls on the Proberts and her question gives opportunity for Francie Dosson's portrait and beauty to be described. *The Reverberator*

DOUVES, BLANCHE DE: Sister of Raoul. Her kleptomania is one of the scandals published in the *Reverberator* that are so painful to the Proberts. *The Reverberator*

DOUVES, M. DE (RAOUL): Marries Jane Probert. The most countrified but the most genuinely traditional in manner and style of life of the family: a very small black gentleman with thick eyebrows and high heels (wears sabots on his country estate). Is suspected of thinking he resembles Louis XIV. *The Reverberator*

DOUVES, MME. DE (JANE, JEANNE): The largest, heaviest of the Proberts, lives in La Vendée, where she is considered majestic in spite of her old clothes that justly make her seem a figure from the past. Though at first formidable she seems essentially comforting to Francie Dosson, and is an excellent woman, though seeing people and situations in terms of relationships and alliances. *The Reverberator*

DOVEDALE, LORD: Captain Lovelock's elder brother; has seven

children and three governesses, but, having paid Lovelock's debts seven times already, when applied to for money sends only a letter of good advice. *Confidence*

DRAKE, MR.: Lord Rye's butler. Mrs. Jordan's engagement to him to save herself from want punctures her fantasies of equality with the nobility and amazing success in her career. *In the Cage*

DREUIL, COMTE DE: A Frenchman who talks twaddle at the Newmarch house party. *The Sacred Fount*

DREUIL, COMTESSE DE: The comte's American wife—too much 'all there' to be the hypothetical mistress who has transferred all her own wit to Gilbert Long. *The Sacred Fount*

DUCHESS, THE (JANE): A distant cousin of the Brookenhams, though apparently of European background and widow of a Neapolitan. Disapproves of many English customs for their vagueness, especially the upbringing of girls like Nanda Brookenham. Childless, she is educating her husband's niece Aggie on the Continental system of total worldly ignorance and constant supervision. Succeeds in marrying her to the very rich Mr. Mitchett, and is obviously very alarmed at Aggie's immediate plunge into fast behaviour, particularly in her attraction of the Duchess's own lover, the formerly paternal Lord Petherton. For all her experience, she seems to have believed in some real innocence behind the imposed surface of ignorance. *The Awkward Age*

DUKE, THE: The important figure who as 'a very bad institution' is selected as the target of Hyacinth Robinson's assassination attempt. *The Princess Casamassima*

DUNOYER, MLLE.: Accomplished actress at the Théâtre Français, the celebrated, the perpetual, the necessary ingénue, 'who with all her talent could not have represented a woman of her actual age.' Her polished professionalism fascinates the untried Miriam Rooth. *The Tragic Muse*

E

EGBERT, LORD: A prig whom Mr. Carteret may, it is suggested, wish Nick Dormer to resemble. *The Tragic Muse*

ERIC, LORD: One of Ida Farange's many admirers or lovers, though another of them, the Captain, identifying him as 'what-do-you-call him's brother, the fellow that owned Bobolink' denies she ever knew or looked at him. *What Maisie Knew*

EUGENIO: A tall handsome Italian with superb whiskers, the Millers' courier in Europe, who rather despises their casual household. Is greatly admired by the Millers and their admiration is considered vulgar by more sophisticated compatriots. *Daisy Miller*

EUGENIO: An Italian courier and master of household employed by Milly Theale for her visit to Venice. With his thick white hair, smooth fat face and black, professional, almost theatrical eyes, he is extortionately expensive, but performs his job magnificently. Despises Milly's suitor, Merton Densher, whose interest is less straightforwardly mercenary. *The Wings of the Dove*

EVERARD, CAPTAIN: Also signs himself Philip, William and even Mudge on the telegrams he is constantly sending so that the Telegraphist at his local Post Office becomes imaginatively involved through them in his secret love affair with Lady Bradeen. Delicate enough to appreciate the Telegraphist's romantic but not vulgar attitude during their one personal encounter, he seems to become more emotionally interested in her after she dextrously saves him from scandal by recalling verbatim a compromising telegram, and as his love for Lady Bradeen wanes with the necessity of marrying her, the Telegraphist prudently moves out of the district and his life. *In the Cage*

EVERS, BLANCHE: A very pretty, very American young girl, but sillier and more coquettish than most. Her distinction is a constant flow of inconsequential, amusing chatter, much admired by the indulgent. Marries Gordon Wright who deliberately decides that this sort of naïvety is what he wants.

Disliking his sober behaviour she begins flirting to provoke greater attentiveness, he reacts with further withdrawal, and eventually Blanche finds herself on the brink of an unenthusiastic elopement with her girlhood flirt, Lovelock. Here the Vivians exert their influence to reconcile her with her husband and wifely duties. *Confidence*

EVERS, MRS.: An old friend of Mrs. Vivian to whom she confides her frivolous daughter, hoping Mrs. Vivian's 'lovely' influence will affect her—a hope tardily realised just in time to save Blanche's marriage. *Confidence*

F

FARANGE, BEALE: A glittering well-dressed man who appears over-crowded with jewellery and flowers, permanently garnished with his vast fair beard and the eternal glitter of his teeth. After a brief unpaid period with a legation he lives unoccupied and precariously on his twenty-five hundred. Being divorced from his wife Ida he is given custody of their child Maisie but because he has misappropriated Ida's large provision for Maisie's maintenance his custody is modified to give her six months with each parent in turn. Attracted to Ida's beautiful governess Beale eventually marries her, coming later to dislike and desert her too for an ugly but very rich American 'countess'. His final, typical coup is to manoeuvre Maisie into refusing his insincere offer of a home, vanishing from her life for good. *What Maisie Knew*

FARANGE, IDA: Later known as 'her ladyship'. A lady of brilliant complexion, dubious morals and, when necessary, tremendous charm; her mouth and waist are tiny, her eyes huge, 'like Japanese lanterns swung under festal arches.' Very tall, she has long arms that promote her public excellence at billiards. She and her divorced husband Beale use their daughter Maisie as a weapon without compunction. Ida marries the younger Sir Claude but later has a succession of lovers, eventually taking a formal farewell of Maisie whose innocent comment on her multitudinous affairs spoils her martyred pose. Unpredictable and tempestuous—even her wrath being 'a thing of resource and variety'—she occasionally reveals mysterious (to Maisie) depths of charm and emotion. *What Maisie Knew*

FARANGE, MAISIE: A little girl divided six months at a time between her parents Ida and Beale. At first unconscious of her parents' use of her to carry insults, she evades this role, upon recognising it, by feigning stupidity. Liking however to keep the peace she accepts uncritically the most raffish features of her life, such as her governess Miss Overmore's accompanying her to Beale's house (against Ida's orders) only to neglect her there for Beale's society. This is compensated by Ida's next governess for her, Mrs. Wix, who is kind, safe, ugly and unqualified. As Miss Overmore marries Beale and becomes 'Mrs. Beale' she no longer claims to carry on Maisie's education at Beale's home, but, drifting apart from Beale and meeting through Maisie Sir Claude, Ida's second husband, she takes Maisie to the 'courses' and 'lectures' he has suggested mainly in the hopes of meeting him there. Maisie far prefers her stepparents to whom her real ones now virtually abandon her, but as well as their genuine affection for her they wish to 'use' her as window-dressing for their projected new home abroad. Though little aware of the conventional view, as urged by the faithful Mrs. Wix, Maisie suspects the reliability of the susceptible stepparents, and when neither will renounce the other to care for her alone, she leaves with the limited, conventional but safe Mrs. Wix. *What Maisie Knew*

FARANGE, THE SECOND MRS.: *see* Beale, Mrs.

FARRINDER, AMARIAH: Mrs. Farrinder's husband. *The Bostonians*

FARRINDER, MRS.: A copious, handsome woman, with glossy black hair and a terrible regularity of feature. Famous as a lecturer, she speaks slowly and distinctly at her own inexorable pace, and her aims are 'to give the ballot to every woman in the country and to take the flowing bowl from every man.' Very strong-willed indeed, she withdraws her original patronage of Verena Tarrant and Olive Chancellor, possibly from jealousy, possibly from dislike of their romantic approach to the women's rights cause, and as her disapproval weighs heavily, so her witnessing Verena's final desertion of the public platform is the culminating bitterness for Olive. *The Bostonians*

FEATHERSTONE, MISS: An English lady who meets the Millers on a train in Europe: her wondering why Daisy Miller does not give lessons herself to her little brother shows a European misunderstanding of the American Daisy's type and way of life. *Daisy Miller*

FENTON, GEORGE: A Western cousin of Nora Lambert, with black hair, keen dark eyes and tough maturity, though only twenty-five, having dabbled in affairs and adventures since he was ten. His introduction of himself to Nora and her guardian Roger Lawrence is based on his instinct to make money out of everything. Shrewd and eager, he somehow lacks some element of success—vanity makes him refuse money as he is being sent away by Roger. However by the time Nora seeks refuge with him after rejecting Roger's proposal of marriage, he has deteriorated beyond romantic vanity: his plan to imprison and ransom her to Roger reveals his turpitude and his inability to accomplish even this reveals his weakness. *Watch and Ward*

FEUILLET, M. OCTAVE: The author of a story in a French review. *The Princess Casamassima*

FILER, MR.: A large, heated-looking man, an impresario of public lectures and lower entertainments, and agent employed by Olive Chancellor to promote Verena Tarrant's great Boston public appearance. He curses and threatens legal action when she elopes with Basil Ransom instead of performing. *The Bostonians*

FILOMENA: Mme. Grandoni's old washerwoman, a greater lady than Mrs. Light, in her employer's opinion. *Roderick Hudson*

FINCH, DR.: A New York doctor, forerunner of Sir Luke Strett in attending Milly Theale just before she leaves for Europe. His way of not saying anything important raises misgivings, later fulfilled. *The Wings of the Dove*

FINCH, MISS DORA: An American in Paris, friend of the Tristrams. Her amazingly shrill continuous conversation makes Newman consider her good as a warning, like the gong that sounds for dinner. *The American*

FINUCANE, LORD: An Irish peer whose estates are transmitted through his only child Lady Bridget to her son Lord Deepmere. *The American*

FIRMIN, MRS.: A guest at Waterbath, as dreadfully devoid of taste as the rest, but no danger to the marriageable Owen Gereth as she is married already. *The Spoils of Poynton*

FLACK, GEORGE: A typical young American reporter, whose appearance is too typical to allow him any individuality of feature. Self-centred, energetic and honest by his own lights, his objectives in Paris are to relay interesting gossip to his paper the *Reverberator*, and to marry beautiful, rich Francie Dosson. Refused by her, he returns later to find her engaged to Gaston Probert, an engagement he endangers by publishing Francie's gossip about the Proberts. He cannot understand their horror at this, and his steam-rollering faith in publicity is eventually rejected by Francie as she sees the distress it can cause. *The Reverberator*

FLORA, OR FELICIA, LADY: The aristocratic lady—her name is only vaguely known—to whom Lord Warburton is said to be engaged. *Portrait of a Lady*

FLORA, LADY AND ELIZABETH, LADY: Members of Nick Dormer's family, possibly sisters of his mother Lady Agnes. Mrs. Lendon enquires ceremoniously after them. *The Tragic Muse*

FLORA: Eight-year-old sister of Miles, former pupil of the governess Miss Jessel, who has been corrupted by the valet Quint. The new Governess, believing that these two now dead are appearing as ghosts to her and the children, fails to win Flora back, so that she lapses from beautiful innocence into hysteria, bad language and physical illness. This provides an excuse for sending her away from the evil influence of her home, and the Governess hopes she may thereafter recover. *The Turn of the Screw*

FLORINE OR DORINE: *see* Topping, Miss

FOAT, MRS. ADA T. P.: Celebrated trance-lecturer, speaks on 'the Summer-land'; her photograph shows her with a surprised expression and innumerable ringlets. Dr. Tarrant has, his wife suspects, been 'associated' with her when both belonged to the matrimonially experimental Cayuga community, and she is typical of the second-rate charlatanism of the Tarrants' circle. *The Bostonians*

FRANÇOIS: Waiter at Strether's pension, who strikes Strether as not only a man and a brother but also as typifying the atmosphere of Paris. *The Ambassadors*

FRANKS, MR.: A small meagre man with some kind of epileptic affliction, George Fenton's improbable partner. Franks has supplied the capital for their business and is not satisfied with it. *Watch and Ward*

FREZZOLINI, MME.: A celebrated singer whom Newman suggests engaging for his party, a celebration of his betrothal preempted by the old Marquise de Bellegarde. *The American*

FRITZ: Referred to in Lady Bradeen's telegram. *In the Cage*

FROOME, MRS.: Her affair with Lord Lutley is an accepted, 'grandmotherly', almost conventional feature at the Newmarch house party. *The Sacred Fount*

FROTHINGHAM, MISS: Lady Davenant's maid. *A London Life*

G

GARLAND, MARY: A second cousin of the Hudsons, all of whose male relations are ministers of religion. Usually grave in expression, her irregular features are charming if not pretty, and she is evidently a girl of great personal force, though lacking pliancy. Attracted by his fire and genius she becomes engaged to Roderick Hudson just before Rowland Mallet takes him to Rome to become a sculptor: she visits him there with his mother two years later, hoping to counteract his moral deterioration and infatuation with Christina Light. Unlike Roderick's mother she is grateful, not resentful of Rowland's efforts on behalf of her fiancé. But far from returning Rowland's secret love for her, she is undeterred by

Roderick's errors, indifference and even his eventual demand for money to pursue the now married Christina. Any anger is eclipsed by her anxiety and anguish at his disappearance and death while out climbing. In spite of her sense and generosity, her reserve about her feelings prevents Rowland being too hopeful of winning her even in the distant future. *Roderick Hudson*

GARLICK, MR.: Well-protected Aggie attends his classes in modern light literature, though her aunt is a little nervous about the subjects. *The Awkward Age*

GELSOMINA: Aggie's old maid, her former nurse. *The Awkward Age*

GEMINI, COUNT: A nobleman of ancient Tuscan family but small estate, marries Amy Osmond for her modest fortune, though he later inherits money. A 'low-lived brute', he gives his wife every excuse for her frivolity and infidelities. *The Portrait of a Lady*

GEMINI, COUNTESS (AMY): Née Osmond. A restless, gaudily dressed, exotic, bird-like woman. She has a great deal of manner though her morals are less substantial—her excuse being the horrible and unfaithful Italian husband to whom her mother has foolishly married her. Sister of Gilbert Osmond, whom she dislikes for his heartlessness, she regrets his marriage to Isabel Archer and later promotes their separation by revealing his former love affair and continuing association with Madame Merle, real mother of his child Pansy. *The Portrait of a Lady*

GERETH, COLONEL: Soldier brother of the late Mr. Gereth, good-naturedly lends his widowed sister-in-law and nephew his rather tasteless house in Cadogan Place for May and June. *The Spoils of Poynton*

GERETH, MR.: Husband of Mrs. Gereth for twenty-six years, during which he has shown sympathy, generosity and love, and shared with her a mutual passion for seeking out beautiful treasures for their house Poynton. Nevertheless he leaves her only a cottage and small income, and the house and all their acquisitions go to their philistine son Owen. *The Spoils of Poynton*

GERETH, MRS. ADELA: A fresh, fair widow lady looking young for fifty, whose life and devotion are bound up in her home, Poynton, and the treasures she has been collecting all her married life; but her husband has left all this to their son Owen who becomes engaged to the robust, determined and completely philistine Mona Brigstock. Fighting to prevent the marriage and also to retain what she can from Poynton, Mrs. Gereth uses her sensitive and intelligent protégée Fleda Vetch as intermediary, hoping Owen will somehow fall in love with Fleda instead. This indeed happens after he has an ugly disagreement with Mona, provoked by Mrs. Gereth's flight to her dower house with several wagon-loads of Poynton's best treasures. However her moral blackmail of Fleda, pressing her to take possession of Owen (effected by returning the treasures to Poynton for her) is defeated by Fleda's scrupulous waiting for Owen's formal freedom, and Mona's unscrupulous pounce on him, somehow forcing him suddenly to marry her. Clever enough in manipulating her treasures, Mrs. Gereth perhaps allows them to dominate human relationships: however she cares more for their appreciation than mere possession, and even after thus losing them because of Fleda's scruples, she generously insists on Fleda's living with her, as they share common tastes, memories, and griefs. *The Spoils of Poynton*

GERETH, OWEN: Heir to Poynton, handsome, heavy and honourable, he seems to Fleda Vetch 'absolutely beautiful' and 'delightfully dense'. As such he is uncomfortable between his mother, who carries off more of the treasures of Poynton than the letter or spirit of the law permits, and his fiancée Mona Brigstock who demands he get the treasures back before they marry. After the selfish claims of both, he comes to appreciate the delicate honour of Fleda, and falls in love with her. However his dislike of unpleasantness is a real weakness, for his trip to break officially with Mona ends in her forcibly marrying him. He then apparently sinks into happy domesticity, except that he wants to give one of Poynton's best treasures to Fleda: but like the treasures, largely destroyed in a sudden fire, his future is only a shadow of what it might have been. *The Spoils of Poynton*

GIACOSA, THE CAVALIERE GIUSEPPE: Accompanies Mrs. Light and her daughter Christina in their wanderings in Europe;

he runs errands and fights off their creditors. A little elderly man, shabbily but carefully dressed, with small glittering eyes and a short, stiff white moustache. His faultless urbanity gives the effect of 'a little waxen image whose soul has leaked away'. His anxious social ambitions for Christina—and his paradoxical admiration of her nobler rebellion against social ambition—are explained by the secret that he is her father. *Roderick Hudson*

GILMAN, MR.: The minister of the church attended by the Wentworths. His sermons are 'always pleasant'. *The Europeans*

GIOVANELLI, MR.: A handsome young Italian who becomes Daisy Miller's constant escort in Rome, creating a very bad impression in respectable society: his intention, as in taking her to the Colosseum one unhealthy night, may have been to compromise and marry her: he admits at her graveside that she was the most innocent of ladies. *Daisy Miller*

GLORIANI: In *The Ambassadors*: not the same Gloriani as in *Roderick Hudson*. Italian by birth, a famous sculptor with a fine, worn, handsome face. Not only his distinguished career and already priceless works, but the tremendous inclusive intelligence of his glance strike Strether as an ultimate standard. At one of Gloriani's distinguished 'at homes' Strether first meets the Vionnets. *The Ambassadors*

GLORIANI, MME.: In *The Ambassadors*: not the same Mme. Gloriani as in *Roderick Hudson*. Wife of the sculptor, whose somewhat massive majesty melts, at any contact, into the graciousness of some incomprehensible tongue. *The Ambassadors*

GLORIANI: In *Roderick Hudson*: not the same as Gloriani in *The Ambassadors*. An American sculptor of about forty, of European extraction and residence. A great talker and a picturesque one, being bald with a small bright eye, a broken nose and a waxed moustache. After spending a large fortune recklessly and quickly, he lives by his talent to produce a corrupt effect of mingled beauty and vileness, which, being intended to fascinate and puzzle, is the opposite of Roderick Hudson's ideal of presenting pure beauty. *Roderick Hudson*

GLORIANI, MME.: In *Roderick Hudson*: not the same as Mme.

Gloriani in *The Ambassadors*. A lady with a plain face, living with Gloriani but not in fact his wife. *Roderick Hudson*

GOLDIES, THE: Some of the English people who are the friends of the Misses Bordereau in their period of comparative sociability. *The Aspern Papers*

GOODWOOD, CASPAR: The earliest of Isabel Archer's suitors, to whom, having encouraged him, she feels some guilty obligation. A straight young man from Boston, whose angular jaw, fixed blue eyes and conventional, too new clothes bespeak his uncompromising ruthless, driving character. He persists in his suit against all discouragement, and the blow of Isabel's marriage to Gilbert Osmond ages him, but on learning of her unhappiness he urges her to leave her husband and return to America with him. His singlemindedness, as much as his general harshness of character, frightens Isabel into rejoining her husband, although her only prospect is conflict. *The Portrait of a Lady*

GORHAM: Little Effie Bream's massive, formidable nurse who disapproves of unwholesome, rich foods at 'the other house'. The cause of Effie's death is kept from her. *The Other House*

GOSTREY, MARIA: A brown, thin American lady, expensively but reticently dressed, wears spectacles and has delicately greying hair. Befriends Lambert Strether, a fellow traveller from America, and bestows on him her experience—it is her hobby—of introducing Americans to Europe and its culture, especially in Paris, now her home. Thus Strether, instead of fulfilling his mission to bring home his young compatriot Chad Newsome, becomes more appreciative of Paris even than she is. She knows, but does not betray, the passionate love affair underlying Chad's ambiguous attachment to her old schoolfriend, Mme. de Vionnet. Though Strether's growing affection for her supersedes his reverential attachment to his fiancée Mrs. Newsome, and even survives his dazzlement by Mme. de Vionnet, he resists her invitation to remain in Paris and let their relationship grow—he has to renounce her to prove his disinterestedness. Her attitude to Paris, less roseate than Strether's and less rapacious than Chad's, is like her attitude to life: she is the ideal confidante and mentor. *The Ambassadors*

GOUGENHEIM, PROFESSOR: Destined to speak on the Talmud to a New York ladies' association, which holds evening meetings to promote culture and intellectual improvement. *The Bostonians*

GOVERNESS, THE: A clergyman's daughter who while looking after two charming mysterious children Miles and Flora, sees the ghosts of their former governess Miss Jessel and her lover Quint trying to exert an evil influence. Although the housekeeper Mrs. Grose helps by taking the demoralised Flora away, the Governess tries to win over Miles, who in the conflict suddenly dies. An intense, serious person, she dedicates herself perhaps obsessively to defeating the ghosts that only she sees. *The Turn of the Screw*

GRACIE, MR.: A hard-headed, cynical New Englander, short and unkempt looking, he is wittier and shrewder than his fellow-student Henry Burrage, whom he first introduces to Verena Tarrant. *The Bostonians*

GRANDONI, MME.: An excessively ugly old German lady of ancient family; widow first of a German archaeologist, she makes the mistake of remarrying a music master, who beats her and then leaves her. She has however otherwise great good sense, thirty years of experience of Roman society, a fund of Teutonic sentiment and real kindliness which equip her as Miss Blanchard's occasional chaperone in Rome and later as Christina Light's confidante. After Christina's marriage to and separation from Prince Casamassima she lives with her as companion and insurance of respectability both to the world and to the Prince: she leaves Christina finally because of the younger woman's involvement in revolutionary activity rather than her immoral behaviour. Goes to live with the Prince, her sympathy resting eventually with him. *Roderick Hudson* and *The Princess Casamassima*

GRANDONI, MAESTRO: The Neapolitan music master, husband of Mme. Grandoni, ten years younger than she is, who eventually runs off with a *prima donna assoluta*. *Roderick Hudson*

GRANTHAM, MRS.: The stepmother of Julia Bream. She has terrorised her second husband, and made her stepdaughter's and first husband's lives a misery, so that her visit provokes the dying Julia to insist that her husband vows never to give their baby daughter a stepmother. *The Other House*

GREEN-ERIN, DUKE OF: His conduct to the Butterworths figures in a warning tale told by Mrs. Westgate to illustrate the snobbish contempt of the English aristocracy for visiting Americans from whom they have received favours in America. *An International Episode*

GREENSTREET, ABRAHAM: Mrs. Tarrant's father, a celebrated abolitionist, who dies leaving very little money, having spent his modest fortune helping slaves. *The Bostonians*

GRENDON, MR.: Tishy's inadequate husband. *The Awkward Age*

GRENDON, MRS. TISHY: A pretty, rather silly young woman who wears fashionable dresses of sometimes breathtaking impropriety. Her friend Nanda Brookenham visits Tishy constantly with her mother's encouragement so that she does not get in the way at home. However Tishy's rather fast style of life and greater worldly experience are considered by many unsuitable for her young friend, and though Nanda's own knowledge of the world has been early acquired in the casual Brookenham household, it is probably seeing her in Tishy's raffish circle of friends that decides Vanderbank against marrying her. *The Awkward Age*

GRESHAM, MRS.: A married woman 'usually taken for a widow mainly because she was perpetually "sent for" by her friends and her friends never sent for Mr. Gresham.' Discreetly dressed for the semi-administrative functions she performs, she chaperones Julia Dallow against Nick Dormer (or her own weakness) after Julia has jilted him. 'No-one had ever discovered whether anyone else paid her.' *The Tragic Muse*

GRIFFIN, MR.: A revolutionary little shoemaker with red eyes and a greyish face, terribly in earnest, who frequents the anarchist gatherings at the Sun and Moon public house. *The Princess Casamassima*

GRIFFIN: Guest at a country house party. His story of a ghost appearing to a child prompts Douglas to tell the story of Miles and Flora. *The Turn of the Screw*

48

GRIFFIN, MRS.: Fellow guest and listener to Douglas's ghost story. *The Turn of the Screw*

GRINDON, MR.: Only son of an immensely rich industrial and political baronet in the North, anxious to marry Biddy Dormer; being thoroughly discouraged by her, he at once marries Lady Muriel Macpherson. *The Tragic Muse*

GROSE, MRS.: Housekeeper at Bly, a stout, simple, plain, clean, wholesome woman who looks after little Flora until the new Governess arrives. She describes the supervision of Flora and her brother Miles by the corrupt former governess Miss Jessel and her lover the valet Quint, both now dead. At first she only reluctantly accepts the new Governess's account of their continuing ghostly influence, but is later convinced by the dramatic deterioration into vulgarity and grossness by Flora, whom she then thankfully takes away from the evil atmosphere of the house. *The Turn of the Screw*

GROSJOYAUX, M. DE: A short, stout, fair man with an air of gay surprise, who acts as Valentin de Bellegarde's second in his fatal duel. *The American*

GROSPRÉ, M. DE: Among the guests of Mme. de Brécourt whose brother Gaston Probert prefers to dine with the newly-met Dossons. *The Reverberator*

GRUGAN, ROKER AND HOTCHKIN: Three of Hyacinth Robinson's fellow workmen at Crookenden's. Good-natured, limited fellows, who are jealous of neither his small legacy from Miss Pynsent nor his invitations from their master's family. *The Princess Casamassima*

GUSHMORE, MR.: A London man who 'chops down' a French play to make it suitable for London audiences as Miriam Rooth's first vehicle. *The Tragic Muse*

GUSSY: Referred to in Lady Bradeen's telegram. *In the Cage*

GUTERMANN-SEUSS, MR.: A remarkably genial, positively lustrous young man, of apparently less than thirty summers yet father of eleven progeny, as he confesses without a sigh. A Jewish dealer in antiquities, he invites Adam Verver to his home to view (and eventually buy) certain priceless antique tiles. *The Golden Bowl*

H

HADDON: Referred to in Lady Bradeen's telegram. *In the Cage*

HARRINGTON, CATHERINE: *see* Sloper, Mrs. Catherine

HATCH, C. P.: An American in Paris, friend of the Tristrams. *The American*

HAYCOCK, LORD: Husband of the radical Lord Warburton's elder sister: 'a very good fellow but unfortunately a horrid Tory'. *The Portrait of a Lady*

HENNING, MILLICENT: Childhood sweetheart of Hyacinth Robinson, whom she revisits after emerging triumphantly from her family's plunge into wretchedness and squalor. Partly luck, partly her robust, unassailable beauty, health and confidence (all typically and evidently cockney) have established her as a successful model-cum-saleswoman in a large store. Hyacinth's sympathy for his fellow cockneys, as well as her beauty, draws him to her; but his love for the refined Princess Casamassima and Millicent's practical awareness of his poverty prevent serious courtship. However his attempt to find refuge from both the Princess's fickleness and the urgency of his political involvement, in Millicent's familiar affection is thwarted by her obvious attachment to the effete, worthless but fashionable and rich Captain Sholto. *The Princess Casamassima*

HENNING, MR.: Father of Millicent, a poor man, supposed to fill a position of confidence in a brush factory. *The Princess Casamassima*

HENNING, MRS.: A mother and housewife deficient in economy and sobriety, whose relations with a stove-polisher off Euston Road are no secret from her neighbours. Dies suddenly, after the family have left Lomax Place. *The Princess Casamassima*

HILARY, MR.: Mr. Touchett's solicitor. *The Portrait of a Lady*

HODGE, D. JACKSON: A typical American name as seen on luggage in the Dossons' hotel. *The Reverberator*

HOFFENDAHL, DIEDRICH: Famous anarchist, the only leader captured after an important European uprising, who never betrays his friends through twelve years' pressure and imprisonment. He is secretly organising a new campaign of terror in which Hyacinth Robinson promises to assassinate a prominent figure. Though corresponding with the Princess Casamassima, who sees him as the 'genius of a new social order', he evidently does not rely on her revolutionary fervour. *The Princess Casamassima*

HOPE, SIR MATTHEW: A great London doctor who visits Mr. Touchett at Gardencourt. Ralph Touchett, however, has more faith in the local doctor and in his own final illness has Sir Matthew's visits stopped. *The Portrait of a Lady*

HOPE, SIR MATTHEW: A great doctor; visits Mr. Carteret twice in one week. *The Tragic Muse*

HOPPUS, MR.: Author of a political article in a political journal. Julia Dallow's liking for this article and Nick Dormer's indifference to it on the occasion of his proposing marriage to her indicate a threatening divergence of interests. *The Tragic Muse*

HUDSON, MR.: A Virginia landowner, father of Roderick, who turns out a dreadful rake, squanders his own and his wife's fortunes, and drinks himself to death. *Roderick Hudson*

HUDSON, RODERICK: Born of an impoverished Virginia family, and though spoilt by his widowed mother, he tries to console her for his brother's death by studying law, against his real vocation for sculpture. His talent is discovered by the prosperous, benevolent and unoccupied young connoisseur Rowland Mallet, who takes him to Rome to study and work. Volatile, tempestuous and enthusiastic, Roderick responds passionately to Rome and produces some works of real genius, only to fall equally enthusiastically in love with the beautiful Christina Light, in spite of being engaged already to his cousin Mary Garland. Christina's complex character and her ambitious mother's opposition to moneyless suitors work havoc on Roderick's character. When deserted by artistic inspiration he proves to have no other resources—no will-power, independence or sense of duty. Unappreciative of Rowland's financial support, he is also ungracious during the visit of his mother and Mary Garland. Ready to pursue Christina again, though she is by now married, he is finally shaken by learning of Rowland's secret unselfish love for Mary: their quarrel is followed by his fall to his death during a mountain walk. Always spontaneous and sincere, especially in his egotism, it is characteristically with his own inartistic failure to perceive his benefactor's feelings that he reproaches himself—still with no thought for the feelings themselves. *Roderick Hudson*

HUDSON, MRS. SARAH: A timid, still youthful widow who clings to her surviving younger son Roderick and only reluctantly allows him to leave his safe but uncongenial law studies to become a sculptor in Rome. There is 'no space in Mrs. Hudson's tiny maternal mind for complications of emotion' and she blames his benefactor Rowland Mallet for taking him to Rome, ignoring her son's faults and further deterioration. After his death she will not see Rowland. *Roderick Hudson*

HUDSON, STEPHEN: Roderick's elder brother, a plain-faced, sturdy practical lad who comforts and supports his widowed mother until he dies in the American Civil War. *Roderick Hudson*

I

INGLEFIELD, EARL OF: Father of Lady Aurora Langrish and her seven sisters and three brothers. *The Princess Casamassima*

J

JANE: *see* Duchess, The

JANE, THE HONOURABLE: Daughter of Lord Bottomley. *The Tragic Muse*

JAUNE, MME. DE: A witty, small, crooked woman, nevertheless unfaithful to her husband, whose three sons write to her every day and whose husband has left her all his possessions— unlike her beautiful, virtuous widowed friend Mrs. Gereth, whose menfolk have relegated her to a distant dower house and meagre income. *The Spoils of Poynton*

JESSEL, MISS: Former governess at Bly where she becomes involved in the corruption of her lover the valet Quint, while teaching young Flora. She suffers and eventually dies. The new Governess sees her ghost, pale, haggard but wonderfully handsome, and believes she is still trying to influence Flora. It is the new Governess's appeal to Flora while seeing the apparition that precipitates Flora's breakdown into sudden vulgarity, malice and illness, but with the girl's removal from Bly Miss Jessel is not seen again. *The Turn of the Screw*

JOHN, LADY: Guest at the Newmarch house party, renowned for wit, which she therefore displays ostentatiously and as if under obligation. If some intelligent mistress has transferred all her wit to the initially stupid, now perceptive Gilbert Long, thus exhausting her own resources, then it seems that Lady John cannot be that mistress as she has remained clever. However Grace Brissenden later claims (probably to conceal the fact of her own new love affair with him) that Long is as stupid as ever and involved with Lady John. *The Sacred Fount*

JORDAN, MRS.: Widow of a vicar, well looking (in spite of her large teeth), formerly known to the Telegraphist's family. They meet again during their common descent into abject poverty, and later she and the Telegraphist become friends as they regain comparative prosperity. She does the flower arrangements professionally for society people. Her own imaginary friendships with her clients resemble the Telegraphist's vicarious involvement with her telegraphing customers' affairs, and her marriage, not to Lord Rye (as hinted) but to his butler Drake is a warning to the Telegraphist to be equally realistic and avoid turning her more possible and dangerous fantasies into reality. *In the Cage*

JULIA, LADY: Mother of Mrs. Brookenham. In her day a great beauty, reminiscent of a Gainsborough or even a Raphael subject. Her beauty has been transmitted exactly to her granddaughter Nanda Brookenham, whose character however is more frank and serious—more modern—and who does not benefit from her heredity: modern taste is for a more 'staring, glaring, knockdown' sort of beauty. But Mr. Longdon, Lady

Julia's former suitor first likes Nanda for her own sake. *The Awkward Age*

JULIA, LADY: Lord Lambeth's unmarried sister. *An International Episode*

JUSTINE, MOTHER: An Italian nun, who accompanies Pansy Osmond home from her convent school. *The Portrait of a Lady*

K

KAPP, STANISLAS: Son and heir of a rich brewer of Strasbourg, brawny, bull-headed and rich, who challenges Valentin de Bellegarde to a duel over Noémie Nioche, ungracefully demands a second exchange of bullets, and even more ungracefully, in spite of being 'no shot', wounds him fatally. *The American*

KEITH, MRS. ISABEL: As Miss Isabel Morton she is a fair, plump, pretty woman (though not so pretty as she seems), amiable (though not sympathetic) and clever (though not intelligent). Being keenly ambitious she refuses stolid Roger Lawrence several times, finally and conclusively because she is engaged to another—his despair at this drives him to the eccentric plan of educating the orphan Nora Lambert to be his wife. Later widowed, Mrs. Keith is happier and worthier than before. Satisfied ambition leaves her with no personal interest in Roger, and she undertakes to 'finish' Nora by taking her to Europe. Her prompt criticism when Nora rejects Roger's offer of marriage effects Nora's immediate remorse and eventual change of heart: evidently Mrs. Keith's intelligence and sympathy have developed with maturity. *Watch and Ward*

KEYES, MRS. EDITH: The middle and prettiest Archer sister, she marries an officer of the United States Engineers and ornaments the military stations in the unfashionable West to which she is unwillingly relegated. In their girlhood she always overshadowed her consequently modest sister Isabel. *The Portrait of a Lady*

L

LADLE'S: *see* Simpkin's, Ladle's and Thrupp's

LAMBERT, MR.: A shabby, haggard man of less than middle age; his pretentious foppish moustache contrasts with his harshly lined white face. Approaching Roger Lawrence, a stranger, in a hotel lounge he raves, pleads and demands money, and threatens suicide. When refused money, he carries out this threat, also trying but failing to kill his young daughter Nora, who is then adopted by the pitying and slightly remorseful Roger. *Watch and Ward*

LAMBERT, MRS.: Has been a professional singer. Dies shortly before her husband's suicide. Shown by her portrait as a languid looking lady, and imagined by her daughter's guardian Roger Lawrence as having a gentle long-suffering nature. *Watch and Ward*

LAMBERT, NORA: Left friendless as a child by her father's suicide, she is taken in by Roger Lawrence who plans eventually to marry her. Her Bohemian, scanty education is supplemented by expensive schooling, and Mrs. Keith, whom Roger once wanted to marry, takes her to Europe where she blooms in beauty, intelligence and cultivation. Her grateful affection for Roger is sisterly, however, and she finds more romance in her cousin George Fenton and Roger's cousin Hubert Lawrence. The latter, annoyed at being recalled to duty (and a pre-existent engagement) terminates his flirtation with her rather brusquely, and Nora then refuses Roger's long-meditated, ill-timed proposal. Embarrassed and with some resentment at his interested motives, she flees to New York, giving Fenton and Hubert the chance to show their supposed kindness: both disappoint her, and she realises that familiar, unexciting Roger is the only one with a heart. Appreciating each other fully at last, they marry. *Watch and Ward*

LAMBETH, LORD: A straight, strong, handsome young Englishman, reasonable and competent without being tremendously clever. While staying in Newport, America with Mrs. Westgate, he falls in love with her sister Bessie Alden. During her subsequent visit to England, in spite of (or because of) the disapproving anxiety of his friends, he proposes marriage but is refused. *An International Episode*

LANGRISH, LADY AURORA: One of the eight daughters of the Earl of Inglefield. An original figure whose plain and eccentric appearance—long face, tangled silky hair—hides a passionately sincere desire to better the lot of the underprivileged. She hates her own dull, conventional and useless way of life. Very sensitive to others' feelings, though often gauche through embarrassment, she is in love with the revolutionary young chemical worker Paul Muniment, but realises that his temporary association with the fascinating Princess Casamassima will permanently eclipse her. *The Princess Casamassima*

LAWRENCE, HUBERT: His cleverness and mocking spirit make him a trial to his cousin Roger Lawrence though their differences also draw them together. Hubert becomes a clergyman, with a taste for 'the heavenward face of things' though otherwise decidedly lightweight and wanting in spiritual passion. He mocks Roger's quixotic plan to marry his orphan ward Nora Lambert, but competes for her affection when she grows into a very beautiful woman: he has in fact some hope of escaping the growing superficiality of his life. However he is recalled to discretion (and his prior engagement to Amy, a rich young lady) and leaves Nora abruptly. Her later appeal to him while in temporary distress, to which he cannot respond without outraging the jealous Amy, shows up his disloyal conduct towards both girls. *Watch and Ward*

LAWRENCE, ROGER: Fresh-complexioned and youthful looking, though short-sighted and prematurely bald, he has a tender heart and almost a genius for common sense—but little imagination. Having been rejected frequently by Isabel Morton, he becomes guardian of young Nora Lambert, partly through kindness, partly through guilt at her father's suicide that follows his refusal of money. His tender heart hopes she will love him spontaneously, and his limited imagination fails to prefigure the problems. Anxious and admiring, his affection turns to love as she grows up, but her feelings are of gratitude only and his serious illness, far from arousing her deeper feelings, gives opportunity for the courtship of Roger's romantic cousin Hubert Lawrence. When, recovering, Roger offers marriage, he is rejected. Too generous to let Nora suffer as she hastily leaves for New York, he hurries to find her. She has become disillusioned by the selfishness of supposed friends and admirers, and is ready at last to appreciate his homely but sterling qualities. *Watch and Ward*

LEAVENWORTH, MR.: A tall, expansive, bland American gentleman, with a spacious, fair, well-favoured (but rather blank) face. Very rich, he is travelling to forget his wife's recent death, and patriotically commissions his fellow American Roderick Hudson to sculpt him an allegorical representation of Culture, but this is cancelled when his tactlessness about Roderick's inspiration and private life causes a quarrel. Marries Augusta Blanchard. *Roderick Hudson*

LEBLOND, ABBÉ: Mrs. Keith's confessor, a very charming old man who wishes to convert Nora Lambert to Catholicism. *Watch and Ward*

LEDOUX, M.: A tall, saturnine, grave man, like an old Spanish picture, who once served with Valentin de Bellegarde in the Pontifical Zouaves and acts as his second in his fatal duel. A great Catholic, he is consoled for Valentin's death by the excellent measures for salvation taken on his deathbed. *The American*

LENDON, MRS. URANIA: Mr. Carteret's large, solid, placid sister, a widow living in Cornwall where her great interest is her herbaceous garden. Has already had money from her rich brother, as have her two daughters, and is not greedy for more when summoned to his last illness. *The Tragic Muse*

LIGHT, CHRISTINA: A brilliantly, amazingly beautiful girl. Her character is as complex and varied as her moods, and a strong element of sincere acting directs her behaviour. Never petty nor materialistic, however, she does not favour her mother's plans for a great match with the Prince Casamassima, and though her hopes of true greatness in the sculptor Roderick Hudson are ill-founded, she flirts with him enough to ruin his inspiration and allegiance to his fiancée. Typically, she renounces him for his own good so maddeningly that the result is far worse than the flirtation;

conversely she breaks her engagement to Prince Casamassima with a sincere wish to emulate Roderick's obviously spiritually noble fiancée. However her mother threatens to reveal that her real father is the pathetic, impoverished Cavaliere Giacosa, and to avoid this scandal she marries the Prince. Unhappy in her splendid marriage she feels justified in seizing any pleasure, and meeting Roderick later tempts him to follow her, this being prevented only by his death. For her further career, see Casamassima, Princess. *Roderick Hudson*

LIGHT, MR.: A mild, fair-whiskered young man with some little property, placed as American consul to an Adriatic port, probably to keep him out of harm's way. He marries Miss Savage on impulse, and drowns three years later, no one knows how. Not Christina Light's real father. *Roderick Hudson*

LIGHT, MRS.: Née Savage. Half American and formerly very beautiful though her face can express great fatuity (unlike that of her even more beautiful but clever daughter Christina). Married to an American consul who drowns mysteriously, she later travels in Europe with her former lover Giacosa, Christina's real father, as her courier-cum-servant, expiating upon him 'an hour's too great kindness by twenty years' of contempt'. Obsessed by ambition for her daughter, she gives her a showy, worldly education, and forces her to marry Prince Casamassima by threatening to reveal her illegitimacy. Afterwards retires to Lucca to boast of her achievement. *Roderick Hudson*

LILIENTHAL, MISS: A young German lady, a pianist of merit, engaged twice a week to play duets with her uncle's pupil Nora Lambert. After swearing eternal friendship with Nora one evening over their sweetbread she is sent to the opera in Nora's place, leaving Nora alone with Hubert Lawrence. *Watch and Ward*

LITTLEDALE, CAPTAIN: Mutual friend of the Westgates, Lord Lambeth, and Percy Beaumont; introduces both the latter to the former by letter. Later goes to India and so misses Mrs. Westgate's visit to England. *An International Episode*

LONG, GILBERT: A strikingly handsome, six-foot, curly-haired young man with a big bare blooming face. Originally stolidly stupid, his amazing change from being a 'mere piece of human furniture' to becoming perceptive, cultured and witty is the first mystery of the Newmarch house party; it results from his secret affair with a clever woman, apparently Mrs. May Server, this being betrayed by her corresponding loss of all the wit he has acquired. Long is now neglecting her for Mrs. Grace Brissenden, who has similarly absorbed from her husband all his youth and vitality. *The Sacred Fount*

LONGDON, MR.: A slight, neat, unobtrusive man of over fifty-five, with quick brown eyes, black brows finely marked, and thick, smooth, silver hair: he has 'effect' without 'mass'. Very rich, he returns to London after living retired at Beccles for thirty years, and looks up Vanderbank, whose mother was his first and unsuccessful love, and Nanda Brookenham, whose grandmother Lady Julia was his greatest, also unsuccessful, love. Comes to like Nanda for her own sake, though her modern manners and character at first shock him. Anxious that she marry before becoming too 'battered' by worldly society at home and elsewhere, he offers a large marriage settlement to Vanderbank who after hesitating does not accept. Ironically Mr. Longdon, for all his retirement, comes to realise that Nanda's modern frankness, which becomes risqué gossip in Mrs. Brookenham's salon, is simply honesty; and he eventually carries her away from her family and the dubious influences that she has turned to unappreciated good. *The Awkward Age*

LONGUEVILLE, BERNARD: A clever young man of a contemplative and speculative turn, who nevertheless is a sociable animal. For all his introspection his feelings for Angela Vivian, who is being courted by his friend Gordon Wright, are ambivalent, compounded of mistrust and interest, and eventually he tells Gordon that Angela must be an untrustworthy flirt. Not knowing that Gordon has ignored this, he later feels guilty, especially when meeting her by chance he realises he has always loved her. His engagement to Angela seems calculated treachery to Gordon, now trying to escape from an unsatisfactory marriage and still attracted by her. However by her wisdom and tact she reconciles Gordon to the situation and his wife, and Bernard is spared any tragic results of his hesitations. *Confidence*

LOVELOCK, CAPTAIN AUGUSTUS: A powerful, handsome Englishman, aristocratically connected, with a remarkable auburn beard. His small income and passion for gambling make him a dangerous admirer for Blanche Evers. When he reappears after Blanche's marriage to Gordon Wright, his new nervousness probably results from a sense of being manipulated: Blanche is using him to make Gordon jealous, and Gordon hopes to get rid of Blanche by making her elope with Lovelock. He is left cast off, sore and bewildered by the other characters' happy ending. *Confidence*

LOVICK, EDMUND: One of Peter Sherringham's embassy colleagues, attends the party where Miriam Rooth first appears. *The Tragic Muse*

LOVICK, MRS.: Goodnatured wife of Mr. Lovick and sister of Basil Dashwood, whom she introduces to his future wife, Miriam Rooth. *The Tragic Muse*

LOWDER, MRS. MAUD: A powerful and impressive woman whose very vulgarity is fresh and beautiful. Big, bold, clever and bland, she can afford to like Merton Densher, her favourite niece Kate Croy's suitor, while firmly intending Kate to make a much better match. When Susan Stringham, who knew her as a large florid exotic schoolgirl at Vevey, visits her after many years bringing the beautiful American heiress Milly Theale, Maud not only uses Milly as a social attraction but connives at Kate's pretended matchmaking between Densher and Milly—partly deceived, partly hoping any insincerity may become reality. However Kate is deeper and cleverer than she, and Densher's eventual separation from her is due to other factors, not to Aunt Maud. *The Wings of the Dove*

LUCE, MR.: An American expatriate living in Paris where he frequents the American bankers and the cafés and orders much admired dinners. Confident of enjoying the best possible life in the best possible city, he yet regrets the 'style' of the Napoleonic empire. *The Portrait of a Lady*

LUCE, MRS.: The only person in Paris whom Mrs. Touchett still visits. A colonist since 1830 she reproduces in her well-cushioned little corner of Paris the domestic tone of her native Baltimore. *The Portrait of a Lady*

LUDLOW, EDMUND: New England lawyer with a loud voice and enthusiasm for his profession, who marries Lilian Archer. Regards his original sister-in-law Isabel with wariness rather than admiration. *The Portrait of a Lady*

LUDLOW, JOHN: A clever young lawyer with good prospects who falls seriously and surprisingly in love with Catherine Sloper though she is plain, dull and older than he. But she will not look at him. He afterwards marries the much prettier Miss Sturtevant. *Washington Square*

LUDLOW, MRS. LILIAN (LILY): Eldest of Isabel Archer's sisters, she is 'the practical one' and, being short, solid and plainer than her sisters, is considered lucky to marry at all. Worries about and admires Isabel. *The Portrait of a Lady*

LUDLOWS, THE LITTLE: Mrs. Ludlow's two peremptory little boys, the elder a demonstrative, cheerful child. *The Portrait of a Lady*

LUKE: Servant at Bly; takes letters to the post, etc. *The Turn of the Screw*

LUMLEY, LAURA: An actress who goes on tour to Australia, letting her house to Miriam Rooth. *The Tragic Muse*

LUNA, MR.: Late husband of Mrs. Luna, long-headed enough to settle their son Newton's property on him with safeguards, and large-hearted enough to impose no conditions on his wife's legacy. *The Bostonians*

LUNA, MRS. ADELINE: An attractive widow, over thirty, with clusters of curls, fashionable dresses and a rounded figure. Voluble, rich and conceited, she is 'given up to a merely personal egotistical instinctive life,' unlike her Bostonian younger sister Olive Chancellor. Tries to captivate Basil Ransom, but fails, not only because she is not beautiful or fresh enough, but because he loves Verena Tarrant: her unwise and unsuccessful attempt to keep him from listening to Verena's speech provokes a quarrel and they become enemies. *The Bostonians*

LUNA, NEWTON: Mrs. Luna's son, who is, according to Olive Chancellor, insufferably forward and selfish, spoilt and impertinent, a view confirmed by his tantrums while Basil Ransom tries to give him Latin lessons. *The Bostonians*

LUTCHES, THE MISS (KITTY AND DOTTY): Sisters from the middle West, old friends of Maggie Verver. They stay at the Ververs' country house and feel guilty for bringing with them Mrs. Rance, who begins to pursue Maggie's wealthy and widowed father. *The Golden Bowl*

LUTLEY, LORD: His love affair with Mrs. Froome is an accepted, 'grandmotherly', almost conventional feature at the Newmarch house party. *The Sacred Fount*

M

MACALISTER, MR.: A widower who wishes to make a marriage of reason with the staid, motherly Catherine Sloper, but his genial temperament, handsome features and three little girls fail to attract her. *Washington Square*

MACGEORGE, MR.: A politician cultivated by Julia Dallow; he is certain to be head of some future liberal government. Nick Dormer's coolness to him thus shows political disaffection. *The Tragic Muse*

MACLANE, MISS ELLA: A mutual acquaintance of Blanche Evers and Bernard Longueville whom the latter pretends to remember with insincere but polite rapture. 'Just as interesting as she can be'—her hair comes down to her feet—she is travelling in Europe as far as Norway and Finland, and like Blanche has 'some Englishman' devoted to her. *Confidence*

MACPHERSON, LADY MURIEL: Mr. Grindon shows his frantic (and indiscriminate) determination to marry by proposing to her immediately after failing with Biddy Dormer. *The Tragic Muse*

MADDALENA: A stunted, brown-faced Italian maid at the villa outside Florence hired by the Hudsons. Her brilliant, wolf-like smile flashes at everything in life, especially the things that displease her—her equally enigmatic Italian housekeeping helps distract Mrs. Hudson's anxiety about her son. *Roderick Hudson*

MADDOCK, MISS: The very pretty, typically Irish girl, comes to tea at the Ververs' country house. Hers is the type of beauty in which (unlike Charlotte Stant's) Prince Amerigo's interest is prompt but superficial. *The Golden Bowl*

MAJOR, MRS.: Lives below the Muniments and comes up to make the crippled Rose's bed—has only two beds for her own family of thirteen people. *The Princess Casamassima*

MALLET, MR. JONAS: Father of Rowland, 'a chip of the primal Puritan block, a man with an icy smile and a stony frown,' whose shrewd, silent management of his small unpromising business builds it into a great fortune. Consistent in his puritanical upbringing of his son, he leaves him only a third of his fortune. *Roderick Hudson*

MALLET, MRS.: Née Rowland. A very gentle, compliant woman whose marriage to the rigid Jonas is a mistake, but whose saintly sensibility influences her son. *Roderick Hudson*

MALLET, ROWLAND: A fair-haired, fresh-coloured, large-framed man, heir to a third of his father's substantial fortune. Educated on purposely Spartan principles, he develops a strong sense of duty and moral values, with neither genius, economic necessity nor even strong preferences to guide his efforts. Thus he eagerly devotes his time and surplus money to taking Roderick Hudson, a young sculptor of promise, to Rome, only to be bitterly disappointed when Roderick's brilliant début peters out with the deterioration of his character. His unselfish love for Roderick's fiancée Mary Garland and his guilt for interfering in his life make Rowland patiently bear his protégé's sulks and tantrums until, intolerably provoked, he reveals his love for Mary. Thereafter he feels even guiltier, for Roderick goes for a lonely walk just after this quarrel and falls to his death over a cliff. Rowland's sympathies are engaged by his exact opposite, the selfish, gifted, showy Roderick, but his own solid virtues simply make him suffer the more, as the woman he loves continues to be dazzled by Roderick's lightheartedness. *Roderick Hudson*

MANGER, ALGIE: One of the Manger family, a 'horrid little thing' who is to be paid four hundred a year to 'do his conversation' for the rich Baron Schack, a job Harold Brookenham has pretended he is getting. *The Awkward Age*

MANGER, BOBBY: One of the Manger family, who becomes engaged to the rich American girl whom Harold Brookenham claims he has impressed. *The Awkward Age*

MANGERS, THE: A family coerced into taking Harold Brookenham as a guest for some time. *The Awkward Age*

MANNING: Mrs. Beever's housemaid, who like all her predecessors is in stature, uniform and precision comparable to Frederick the Great's grenadiers—an efficient, shrewd and inexorable person. *The Other House*

MARCHANT, LADY: Wife of a county magnate, who calls with her daughters on the Princess Casamassima at her hired country house. She produces an inexplicable, almost maddening, effect on the princess's nerves. *The Princess Casamassima*

MARCHANT, MISS: One of Lady Marchant's three daughters, an inanimate beauty who does not realise that Princess Casamassima's guest Hyacinth Robinson is only an artisan. She eats three muffins at tea. *The Princess Casamassima*

MARGUERITE: Lady Bradeen's dressmaker, referred to in her telegrams. *In the Cage*

MARIGNAC, MME. DE: Childhood friend of Mr. Probert, she has been instrumental in marrying his daughters into the French aristocracy. Her death leaves him, already widowed, particularly bereft. *The Reverberator*

MARK, LORD: An unemphatic man of indeterminate age, being bald and rather dry (or even stale) but with candid, clear boyish eyes: also indeterminate as to the frivolity, intellectuality or thoughtfulness of his character; and indeterminate even as to talent, with which he is credited on trust rather than on actual achievement. First proposes to Milly Theale and is refused. Later, being refused by her friend Kate Croy, he guesses both girls' interest in Merton Densher. He also guesses Kate's prior secret engagement to Densher, and betrays this to Milly; instead of ingratiating himself by this act, he destroys her will to live. His blind egotism is more culpable than Densher's self-aware, compassionate double game. *The Wings of the Dove*

MARTLE, JEAN: A slim, fair-complexioned girl. It is hoped that her piano playing will become brilliant and her red hair less brilliant. Intended by her distant cousin Mrs. Beevers to marry her son Paul, Jean falls in love with his partner Tony Bream, who had promised his dying wife not to marry while his daughter Effie lives. Jean, unlike her rival Rose Armiger, is devoted to Effie, and it is mainly to incriminate Jean, obviously preferred by Tony, that Rose murders Effie. Distraught by this tragedy, Jean does not believe she can ever marry him now, but is probably wrong. *The Other House*

MASON: Referred to in Lady Bradeen's telegram. *In the Cage*

MERLE, MME. SERENA: A tall, fair, smooth widow of about forty, not pretty though her expression charms: her small grey eyes are full of light and incapable of stupidity. Born in Brooklyn where her father was a naval officer, she has great ambitions but marries the Swiss adventurer, M. Merle. Her love affair with Gilbert Osmond precedes her husband's death, and after it her cooling affection and revived but unsuccessful ambitions keep her single. However when finding her acquaintance Isabel Archer has inherited a fortune she uses her charm to win Isabel's friendship and promote her marriage to Osmond, though neither he nor Isabel thank her as the marriage proves unhappy. Disappointed also in an abortive 'great match' for Osmond's daughter Pansy who is in fact her own daughter by him, and discovered in all these plots and secrets by the disillusioned Isabel, Mme. Merle decides on permanent exile in her native America. Intelligent, talented and perceptive, her main lack is the spontaneous good feeling that Isabel possesses; her calculating self-interest is betrayed by her always guarded manner. *The Portrait of a Lady*

MERRIMAN, MISS: Aggie's governess, entrusted with the constant supervision as well as the education of her charge. *The Awkward Age*

MIDDLETON, MRS.: A very worldly, cynically shrewd old woman who has known Roger Lawrence from boyhood, disapproves of his eccentric 'adoption' of Nora Lambert, and tries unsuccessfully to interest him in the beautiful Miss Sands. *Watch and Ward*

MILES: Left with his sister Flora in the sole charge of the Governess by their uncle. Because of his amazingly beautiful appearance of innocence, purity and freshness, his mysterious expulsion from boarding school puzzles the Governess until she learns of the corrupting influence of her predecessor Miss Jessel and the valet Quint. Both are now dead but appear to her as ghosts trying to affect the children. Eventually she induces Miles to admit the effects and to name Quint, but the conflict and pressure upon him kills him. *The Turn of the Screw*

MILLER, DAISY (ANNIE P.): An American girl travelling with her mother and young brother in Europe. Strikingly, admirably pretty, charming and good-humoured, with a rather monotonous smile and a characteristic ceaseless flow of chatter, she is quite uncultivated and uncomprehending of other societies and their customs. Thus she obstinately follows the customs of her native Schenectady, including independence, forwardness and light flirtation, creating a false impression of defiant promiscuity in Geneva and Rome. Refusing to modify her conduct or abandon her platonic and constant escort Mr. Giovanelli at the advice of others, she finds her reputation ruined even among her stricter compatriots, such as Winterbourne, whom she perhaps loves. Equally stubborn in all respects, she insists on visiting a malarial area of Rome and dies after a short illness. In conflict with a foreign code, her lack of adaptability becomes unexpectedly tragic. *Daisy Miller*

MILLER, EZRA B.: Father of Daisy and Randolph, a very rich businessman who does not accompany his family to Europe. *Daisy Miller*

MILLER, MRS.: Mother of Daisy and Randolph, a small, spare, light person with a wandering eye, a very exiguous nose and a large forehead: vague and ailing, she does not exert authority or guidance over her children so she is no help when the independent Daisy makes a bad impression in strict European society. However she nurses Daisy in her last illness with skill and experience. *Daisy Miller*

MILLER, RANDOLPH C.: An urchin of nine or ten, travelling in Europe with his mother, who restrains him even less than she restrains his elder sister Daisy. He sits up till midnight if he likes. Small, pale, with an aged countenance and voice, he can't wait to return to America. *Daisy Miller*

66

MILLINGTONS, BUNBURYS AND TRIPPS: Mutual acquaintances of Mme. Grandoni and Lady Marchant, which reassures the latter about the social standing of the former. *The Princess Casamassima*

MILLS, LADY: A lady at Milly Theale's Venetian party whose awaited introduction to Densher and her eventual approach punctuates his vital conversation with Kate Croy. *The Wings of the Dove*

MIRANDOLA: A refugee, one of many protected by the philanthropic Miss Birdseye, to whom, in spite of penury, he gives a brooch. *The Bostonians*

MITCHELL, FATHER: A good, holy, hungry man, the trusted and overworked London friend of the Ververs. Enjoys a busman's holiday undertaking the light duties of the Ververs' neighbouring church in the country, staying as their guest. Maggie Verver somehow steers through her problems without consulting him. *The Golden Bowl*

MITCHETT, MR (MITCHY): Outwardly unprepossessing, with prominent eyes, receding chin and violently, ludicrously, deliberately vulgar clothes, he is accepted in Mrs. Brookenham's (and many others') social circle not only because of his immense fortune, gained by his bootmaking family, but because he is unselfish, kind and capable of great generosity. Like Nanda Brookenham he regards the seamy side of life and human nature with matter-of-fact acceptance, but Nanda, whom he loves, will not marry him and persuades him to marry the over-sheltered, innocent Aggie. Having married thus to please Nanda, he is the less hurt by Aggie's sudden plunge into wild, fast behaviour, and he draws support from Nanda's friendship, though she will never allow it to become anything more. Although she worries about him, he is a mature person, ready to endure his fate. *The Awkward Age*

MITCHY: *see* Mitchett, Mr.

MITTON, MR.: Mr. Carteret's solicitor, for whom he sends to disinherit Nick Dormer. *The Tragic Muse*

MODDLE: Maisie Farange's nurse, the safe, regular, typical nanny, who looks after her until she is six or so, but then leaves, either because Maisie is too big for a nurse or because

Moddle has reproved her father Beale for sending insults to his divorced wife via Maisie. *What Maisie Knew*

MOLYNEUX, MILDRED: Younger of Lord Warburton's sisters, with a bright, fresh complexion and something of the smile of childhood. *The Portrait of a Lady*

MOLYNEUX, MISS: Sister of Lord Warburton, extremely sweet and shy, though not in her first youth. Has a smooth nun-like forehead and wears a silver cross. Her simple, subdued goodness intrigues Isabel Archer. *The Portrait of a Lady*

MOLYNEUX, MR.: Vicar of Lockleigh, younger brother of Lord Warburton. He has a big athletic figure, a candid natural countenance, a capacious appetite and a tendency to indiscriminate laughter. Like his sisters he has simple goodness but Isabel Archer doubts his more profound spiritual capacity. *The Portrait of a Lady*

MONTBRON, M. DE: A young man of good family who becomes engaged to Jeanne de Vionnet through traditionally oblique approaches by mutual friends. *The Ambassadors*

MONTENERO: Referred to in Lady Bradeen's telegram. *In the Cage*

MONTGOMERY, MRS.: A small plump fair widow with an extraordinary air of neatness and briskness. Her courage in bringing up five children on a small income and giving money to her selfish brother Morris Townsend is exceeded by her courage in admitting her brother's failings and advising Dr. Sloper against letting him marry his daughter Catherine. *Washington Square*

MORGAN, MRS.: A former unpleasant acquaintance of Mr. Wentworth. Her name is his only association with the term 'morganatic marriage'. *The Europeans*

MOROCCO, PRINCE OF: Said to have been discouraged by the high rent of the apartment Newman later takes. *The American*

MORTON, ISABEL: *see* Keith, Mrs. Isabel

MOSELEY, ELIZA P.: Well-known women's rights speaker: the nine-year-old Verena Tarrant prophetically names her doll after her. *The Bostonians*

MOTCOMB: A friend of Lionel Berrington's, who reports seeing his wife in Paris when she is supposed to be in London. *A London Life*

MUDGE, MR.: Handsome, curly-haired grocery assistant at a Mayfair general Post Office where he becomes engaged to the imaginative lady Telegraphist before moving to a better position in Chalk Farm. Often bores his fiancée unbearably by his calculation, stolidity and predictability, but has courage (deals decisively with drunken brawlers) and generosity (arranges unasked for her drunken mother to share their future home). Respectable, ambitious and practical, he will no doubt go far. *In the Cage*

MUNIMENT, PAUL: A tall, fair, young North-country worker in a London chemical factory: his massive, kindly appearance and uncouth, cheap clothes hide a powerful intellect and ruthless determination. Hyacinth Robinson admires and befriends him and, after joining Paul's anarchist group, enthusiastically volunteers to assassinate an unknown victim. Paul's affection for Hyacinth remains ambiguous, as does the extent of his attraction to the fascinating Princess Casamassima, accepting her contributions while questioning her revolutionary commitment. Nor does he have illusions about the poor he intends to liberate: his convictions are impersonal and unassailable, quite the opposite of Hyacinth's very personal motivation. *The Princess Casamassima*

MUNIMENT, ROSE: Paul's crippled sister, a small, vivacious, dark-haired woman of thirty, wasted by life-long illness. She appreciates the glamour of aristocratic culture as much as Hyacinth Robinson comes to do, though her opposition to her brother's anarchism is perhaps only to tease. Her intellect is as sharp as Paul's and she is similarly ruthless in plotting his success, though for his sake, not for abstract idealism. *The Princess Casamassima*

MÜNSTER, BARONESS EUGENIA CAMILLA DOLORES: A fascinating woman of thirty-three, whose features are individually not beautiful, but who creates somehow the effect of a beautiful woman. Born in Europe of American parents, as a girl she refuses to become the mistress of Prince Adolf of Silberstadt-Schreckenstein but becomes his morganatic wife. When his elder brother wishes to dissolve her marriage for political reasons, she angrily refuses, going to America to strengthen her position, seek her fortune and her mother's relations. Being very fastidious as well as very intelligent she is charmed by the puritan simplicity and solidity of her rich and honest Wentworth cousins, and plans to marry their relation, the even richer Acton. However her project for the sentimental education of her young cousin Clifford Wentworth (wherein she expects more sentiment and intriguing than the young American dreams of) involves her in untruths and disingenuousness that repel the well-travelled but still puritan Acton, and she returns to Europe disappointed. For all her talents and virtues, her values are different from those of her American cousins. *The Europeans*

MUNSTER, MR.: Mr. Dosson's former partner. Gaston Probert takes a letter of introduction to him while transacting business in America. *The Reverberator*

MUNSTERS, THE: A family known to Miss Gostrey but forming a weak link in her introduction to their fellow-voyager Strether as he does not know them well. *The Ambassadors*

MURRAY, MISS: One of Nora Lambert's school teachers. *Watch and Ward*

MURRUM, BISHOP OF: Sits by Mrs. Maud Lowder at her dinner party to which he adds a note of distinctive, unfamiliar Englishness that impresses Milly Theale. *The Wings of the Dove*

N

NARRATOR, THE: An editor and biographer of poet Jeffrey Aspern. After the failure of his fellow editor Cumnor's appeal for information and papers from the aged Juliana Bordereau, Aspern's former mistress, the Narrator poses as a tourist and obtains lodgings in the Bordereaus' house—but makes no progress in spite of winning the sympathy of Juliana's timid, middle-aged niece Tina. Tempted to ascertain if any papers are visible in Juliana's desk, he is caught red-handed when she rises from her sick bed, this shock leading directly to her death. Tina hints that if he married her he would have a right to the papers that she must otherwise destroy, but his obsession abruptly disappears and he feels suddenly that no papers are worth such an unnatural bargain. He reconsiders his decision too late: she has burnt the papers but, sad and meek, bears no malice. *The Aspern Papers*

NARRATOR, THE: At the Newmarch house party he tries to search out the allegiances, experiences and love affairs of his fellow guests, with some confusion, as some—like Guy Brissenden—are unaware of their remarkable changes, and others—like Grace Brissenden—are determined to deceive him. *The Sacred Fount*

NASH, GABRIEL: Former Oxford friend of Nick Dormer's, a fair, fat, bald man with a round face and short beard. After writing a strikingly fine novel he develops a peculiarly individual philosophy of life, chiefly negative in refusing to care for artificial social pressures, but also positive in requiring everyone (everyone, that is, who *is* anyone) to fulfil their vocation—his own being to spot the vocations of others. Thus his influence on Nick Dormer is to encourage his painting and discourage his politics, and though eclipsed by the contrary influence of Julia Dallow, once she withdraws he confirms Nick's distaste for a Parliamentary career. *The Tragic Muse*

NEVILLE-NUGENTS, THE: Apparently Mrs. Rooth's family, though no one else has ever heard of them or their home 'Castle Nugent'. *The Tragic Muse*

NEWMAN, CHRISTOPHER: A tall, lean, brown man in his magnificent prime; in appearance and character a superlative American. As such he comes into tragic conflict with European manners and morals in the persons of the de Bellegarde family, one of whom, the beautiful, gentle, widowed Claire de Cintré, he wishes to marry. Because he is very rich her family agree to leave Claire free to choose, but after he is accepted they have second thoughts, claiming that they need not allow their marriage to follow her 'choice'. Furious at this, Newman learns from the only friendly de Bellegarde, Valentin, of a crime earlier committed by the family. He threatens exposure, but decides that he wants nothing to do with the social world in which they fear exposure and, later, that he will not besmirch himself with ideas of revenge at all. Having suffered Claire's retreat into a closed convent as if it was her death, he at last accepts it as he would accept bereavement. For all his moral superiority to the de Bellegardes, their treachery causes him great suffering. *The American*

NEWSOME, CHAD (CHADWICK): Son of the rich American widow Mrs. Newsome, he goes to Paris as a wild, bold, rough young man and resists summons to return, because, it is rumoured, of involvement with an immoral woman. Strether, his mother's fiancé, is sent to retrieve him but finds him amazingly improved—prematurely grey but possessed of perfect *savoir-faire*, grace, polish and taste. His mistress Mme. de Vionnet has achieved this, but Chad, though grateful, has uneasy longings for a more regular relationship. When he offers to leave her Strether, instead of encouraging him, forbids it. Chad's renewed loyalty to her, proved by arranging her daughter Jeanne's marriage, is none the less suspect, his attachment being the convenional, sophisticated, ultimately superficial one that she, ironically, has familiarised him with. This, and his unexpected fascination with his commercial inheritance, reveal the limitations of polish, beneath which he is still 'only Chad'. *The Ambassadors*

NEWSOME, MR.: Mrs. Newsome's late husband. A man of ideas, he builds up his manufacturing business to greatness, approaching monopoly of the small, vulgar, unnamed household article that he makes. *The Ambassadors*

NEWSOME, MRS.: Gracious, intense, dignified and intelligent widow of a rich manufacturer, she dominates society in Woollett, America. Hearing rumours that an immoral attachment is keeping her son Chad in Paris she sends her fiancé Strether to prove his worth by retrieving Chad. Austere, pure and cool in character, she suspects Strether, and then casts him off, as he seems to think Chad's mistress Mme. de Vionnet can be excused because of the civilising benefits she represents and has conferred on Chad. Strether finally sees his fiancée's impressiveness as a consistent moral and intellectual block—magnificent, but not wholly acceptable. He returns to justify, not reconcile himself to her. *The Ambassadors*

NIOCHE, MME.: M. Nioche's dead wife, who has deceived him greatly, being a flirt like her daughter. *The American*

NIOCHE, M.: A little old Frenchman with a glossy wig and white face: an image of shabby gentility, he has lost both money and confidence. Afraid of his determined daughter Noémie, he expressed his worries about her courtesan's career in high threatening terms, but is last seen obediently carrying her lap-dog. *The American*

NIOCHE, NOÉMIE: Her ambitions to figure in the world keep her copying pictures in the Louvre only until she can encounter a protector to give her a really good start in her courtesan's career. Newman annoys her by being too honourable, but being single-minded she succeeds, destroying *en route* Valentin de Bellegarde, whose fatal duel she encourages to publicise her career. *The American*

NOBLE, MRS.: The Principino's majestic nanny, whose experience is in itself the amplest of pillows and whose attention is a spreading canopy. *The Golden Bowl*

O

OBERT, FORD: A Royal Academician and portrait painter whose awareness of Mrs. May Server's unhappiness, loss of brilliance and over-emphatic pretence of general flirtation alerts the Narrator to her former love affair with Gilbert Long, to whom her brilliance has passed. Obert's final comment that she is 'all right' may or may not mean she has accepted Long's desertion. *The Sacred Fount*

OLIMPIA: The Misses Bordereau's little serving maid, red-haired and white faced, very young and not ugly. Is never accessible enough to provide informative gossip about Miss Bordereau's Aspern papers. *The Aspern Papers*

ORME, LADY AGNES: Referred to in Lady Bradeen's telegram. *In the Cage*

OSMOND, GILBERT: Tall, handsome widower of about forty with a fine, narrow, extremely modelled and composed face,

73

his pointed moustaches and beard suggesting that he is a gentleman who studies style. Although his concealed egotism makes him feel superior to everyone except the Pope and one or two others, his nobly indifferent pose, indeed his whole life, is paradoxically calculated solely to impress the vulgar world. He regards his conquest of the heiress Isabel Archer as public proof of his qualities, but gratitude to his former mistress Mme. Merle for her assistance in this fades as he and Isabel find their common interests are outweighed by their differences. Failing to marry his daughter to Lord Warburton, Isabel's former suitor (for which he blames her), Gilbert forbids her journey to her cousin Ralph Touchett's deathbed. But Isabel discovers just then that Pansy is Gilbert's daughter not by his first wife but by Mme. Merle, and she leaves, not intending to return. Gilbert really idealises the beauty of outward behaviour, and his fine aesthetic perceptiveness and sensitivity make him a formidable opponent in the marital conflict to which Isabel eventually returns. *The Portrait of a Lady*

OSMOND, THE FIRST MRS.: Gilbert Osmond's first wife, who dies soon after their marriage but not, as is claimed, in childbirth: Pansy is in fact the product of Gilbert's very early infidelity with Mme. Merle. *The Portrait of a Lady*

OSMOND, MRS. ('CORINNE'): Mother of Gilbert and the Countess Gemini. Bristling with pretensions to elegant learning she publishes poems and articles and likes to be called 'the American Corinne'. A horrible snob, she has married her daughter to the unpleasant count for his title. *The Portrait of a Lady*

OSMOND, MRS.: *see* Archer, Isabel

OSMOND, PANSY: The small, very pretty daughter of Gilbert Osmond, convent-educated as a perfect 'jeune fille' in being innocent and childlike yet at the same time polished and finished in manners and accomplishments. Left, however, with no sense of her own rights or importance she is easily crushed. Unfortunately, she falls in love with the poor Edmund Rosier and avoids the suit of Lord Warburton, her father's choice; her talent for unobtrusive faithfulness is broken by her father's bland but inexorable banishment to the convent. Her capitulation, realising her own limitations,

74

is her tribute to the truth of things. Frightened by her adored father and Mme. Merle (whom she does not know to be her real mother) she turns to her stepmother Isabel, who partly for Pansy's sake ends her separation from Osmond. *The Portrait of a Lady*

OTTAVIO, DON: Prince Amerigo's Roman cousin, the most 'disponible' of ex-deputies and of relatives, one of those who come to Amerigo's London wedding. *The Golden Bowl*

OVERMORE, MISS: *see* Beale, Mrs.

OWNER OF BLY, THE: A handsome, bold, pleasant, off-hand, gay and kind bachelor, left sole guardian of his orphaned nephew and niece Miles and Flora: his charm dazzles the new Governess into agreeing to educate the children, in spite of his odd condition that, assuming all moral and financial responsibility, she shall leave him totally unconsulted and unconcerned—this condition being more or less essential to allow the later mysteries to develop unchecked. *The Turn of the Screw*

P

PACKARD, GENERAL: An American in Paris, friend of the Tristrams. *The American*

PARDON, MATTHIAS: A young man with precociously white hair, though under thirty. A celebrated Boston journalist who began at fourteen collecting information from hotel registers, he refers all things to print and print to him means simply infinite reporting—the newest thing is always the most interesting. Thus he takes up Verena Tarrant's career as a novelty. Becoming equally struck by her public and private personalities, which he confuses, he wishes to marry her but is refused. *The Bostonians*

PASQUALE: The Venetian servant employed by the Narrator in the hopes that he will elicit information about the Aspern papers from the Bordereaus' maid: in vain, for Pasquale is committed to a Venetian lady bead-stringer who forbids any gossiping with other girls. *The Aspern Papers*

PASQUALE: Milly Theale's brown-faced, silent, efficient gondolier. *The Wings of the Dove*

PAUL, MRS.: George Fenton's landlady, and probably more, to whom he brings his cousin Nora Lambert. Mrs. Paul's role is to persuade her to return to her guardian Roger Lawrence once Fenton has secretly extorted money from him to effect this return, but Nora distrusts her comely, stony face, false smile and artificial ringlets. *Watch and Ward*

PENNIMAN, MR.: Late husband of Dr. Sloper's sister. A poor clergyman of sickly constitution and flowery style of eloquence. *Washington Square*

PENNIMAN, MRS. LAVINIA: Widowed at thirty-three, she settles with her widowed brother Dr. Sloper, ostensibly to be a companion to his daughter Catherine; she is a 'tall, thin, fair, rather faded woman, with a perfectly amiable disposition, a high standard of gentility, a taste for light literature and a certain foolish indirectness and obliquity of character.' Her romanticism leads her to interfere in Catherine's love affair with Morris Townsend, possibly to ill effect, for her calculations tend to encourage his mercenariness. Disappointed in her jilted niece's undramatic behaviour, she none the less continues to be just as officiously romantic, her ringlets and bangles glistening more brightly as she grows older; her failure to reconcile Catherine and Morris after twenty years' estrangement is a real surprise to her. *Washington Square*

PENSIL, LADY: Mr. Bantling's baroness sister. She offers a certain type of English country house life, packed with picnics, sports and theatricals in which, though forty years old and mother of seven, she always plays the principal roles. Supposed to be a 'mastermind', she cannot make out the modern American woman Henrietta Stackpole who is to marry her brother. *The Portrait of a Lady*

PERCIVAL: Student of Archaeology in Paris where his love affair with a young woman who does not expect to marry him shocks his earnest former classmate Babcock, who characteristically searches for excuses for both. *The American*

PERRIAM, MR.: A businessman and millionaire, short, massive, bald, and bushy moustached, with polished little eyes. An admirer or lover of Ida Farange, he eventually 'goes smash' in the City. *What Maisie Knew*

PETHERTON, LORD: A robust man of five-and-thirty with a rather battered face of pleasant brutality: he would have been ugly but for his happy expression, and his voice is unexpectedly cultured and super-civilised. Lives mainly on his rich friend Mitchett and is the lover of the Italian duchess Jane, whose niece Aggie he supervises with fatherly care. However when Aggie marries Mitchett and suddenly becomes a fast socialite, he pursues her, possibly becoming her lover. Though discomfited, Mitchett diagnoses, unconventionally, that Petherton is again probably benefiting Aggie's development. *The Awkward Age*

PIMLICO, COUNTESS OF: Lord Lambeth's pretty, elegant married sister, calls with her mother on Bessie Alden. *An International Episode*

PINKS, MR.: Member of Parliament for Harsh, a constituency controlled by Julia Dallow. His death of heart disease leaves his seat open for Nick Dormer. *The Tragic Muse*

PINTHORPE, MARY: She dines with the Brookenhams. *The Awkward Age*

POCHINTESTA, AVVOCATO: A lawyer still known to the Misses Bordereau, visiting them without fail once a year. He writes beautiful poems and has addressed one to Juliana Bordereau. *The Aspern Papers*

POCOCK, JIM: Small, fat and constantly facetious, straw-coloured and destitute of distinguishing marks, he is a competent businessman but in all other spheres of life features as 'Sally's husband', freely confessing her 'type' to be more developed than his. Accompanying his wife and sister to tempt home Chad Newsome, his brother-in-law, from Paris, he has the opposite effect by exemplifying American small-town vulgarity. *The Ambassadors*

POCOCK, MAMIE: A pretty young American girl, robust, perhaps a trifle too bloodlessly fair, radiant, 'even bridal' (and funny too, 'having never a bridegroom to support her'). Brought to Paris to help retrieve the errant Chad Newsome (for whom she is considered a suitable match) she, more sharply perceptive than the others, recognises the great improvement wrought by Chad's mistress. Seeing there is nothing left to achieve, she is no longer interested in him. When the party leave for Switzerland she has her eye on the rather unenthusiastic Little Bilham. *The Ambassadors*

POCOCK, MRS. SARAH (SALLY): Daughter of Mrs. Newsome, a less refined and less intelligent version of her mother though their physical resemblance is also elusive, Sarah having a longer chin, thin-lipped smile and penetrating voice. Refusing to believe in any good resulting from her brother Chad's immoral love affair in Paris, she does not or will not see the improvement in him. However she develops while in Paris a half-realised flirtation with the patriarchal Waymarsh, so her unrevised condemnation of Chad rings hollow as she leaves. *The Ambassadors*

POUPIN, EUSTACHE: The most brilliant craftsman in book-binder Crookenden's workshop. As an aggressive socialist and constructive democrat 'and a theorist and an optimist and a visionary', he has fled his native France as a political pro-script, but his inflammatory politics are combined with an extraordinary decency of life and worship of proper work. His acquaintance with a chance customer, the more destructive anti-socialist Mr. Vetch, leads to the apprenticeship of Vetch's protégé Hyacinth Robinson at Crookenden's, but Poupin also involves Hyacinth in anarchist circles. *The Princess Casamassima*

POUPIN, MME.: A small fat lady with a bristling moustache, who understands Eustache, his craft and his politics better than he does himself. The closeness of their union strikes their friend Hyacinth Robinson all the more when he learns that they are not formally married. She regards Hyacinth as a son, and is vehemently opposed to his mission of assassination imposed by Eustache's anarchist friends. *The Princess Casamassima*

PRANCE, DR. MARY J.: A plain, spare young woman with short hair and an eyeglass. Without a curve, inflection or grace, she seems neither to ask nor to give odds in the battle of life. Like Basil Ransom she is unconcerned about the rights and responsibilities of women, her own little revolution being a success, but unlike him she regards men and women alike with a drily humorous eye as 'all the same to me' because 'there is room for improvement in both sexes. Neither of them is up to the standard.' An onlooker at Basil's and Olive Chancellor's struggle for Verena Tarrant, she has no wish to fight for women who cannot fight for themselves. Appreciating her shrewdness, Basil takes her on her own terms as a formidable exception to the feminine rule. *The Bostonians*

PREST, MRS.: A benevolent, charitable American living in Venice, the confidante of the Narrator's attempts to extract the Aspern papers from Miss Bordereau. *The Aspern Papers*

PRINCE, THE: *see* Amerigo, Prince

PRINCIPINO, THE: Son and heir of Prince Amerigo and Maggie. *The Golden Bowl*

PROBERT, GASTON: A kind-eyed, smiling youth of American parentage but French birth and upbringing. Falls in love with Francie Dosson whom he meets in his friend Waterlow's studio. As his family value social distinction very highly, he takes great pains to ensure they all approve of Francie, who though rich and beautiful is very uncultivated. Their approval is shattered when she innocently passes on gossip about them to her rejected suitor Flack for publication in his journal, the *Reverberator*. Gaston, also horrified, realises that her mistake shows neither malice nor total insensitivity, but results from different customs and assumptions. Waterlow encourages him to be independent and resist his family, which he eventually does. Not really a weak man, he is imbued by education with European ideas of respect and obedience to the family. *The Reverberator*

PROBERT, MR.: Gaston's American father, an adoptive Parisian whose social position among native Parisians is so distinguished that it is unattainable to transient Americans. His children, born and educated in France, treat him with traditional European deference and respect, so that his acceptance of Gaston's engagement to pretty, rich but uncultivated Francie Dosson is hard won. Naturally the publication of scandal about his family in the *Reverberator* appalls him and Francie's innocent agency in this destroys her credit with him. Not only his authority but Gaston's affection for him make this disagreement very painful. *The Reverberator*

PURVIS, LORD FREDERICK: Lover of Florentine Vivier, whom she stabs to death; the presumed father of her child Hyacinth Robinson. *The Princess Casamassima*

PYNSENT, MISS AMANDA ('PINNIE'): An impoverished dress-maker who brings up Hyacinth Robinson, the illegitimate child of her friend Florentine Vivier. Good-hearted, genteel and sentimental, Miss Pynsent hints at Hyacinth's possible aristocratic paternity, without revealing that Florentine is imprisoned for life for murdering his supposed father Lord Frederick Purvis. However, as her sentimentality also dictates that she must bring the child to Florentine's deathbed as requested, she suffers agonies of self-reproach ever afterwards for Hyacinth's then inevitable discovery of the truth. Her immediate depression brings on an illness from which she never fully regains the physical or mental strength to combat her poverty. Though Hyacinth's absence visiting a princess leaves her final illness unnoticed and neglected until too late, she dies happy in the knowledge of his grand connections and is spared the imminent catastrophe of his political involvement. *The Princess Casamassima*

Q

QUINT, PETER: Former valet to the owner of Bly, a very hand-some, low scoundrel with close-curling red hair, long pale face and strange sharp eyes: left alone with the governess Miss Jessel, and her pupils Miles and Flora, he involves her in his own clever deep corruption. He is found one morning dead beside the road. The new Governess sees the ghosts of him and Miss Jessel, and though she persuades Miles to confess his influence, the strain kills the child. *The Turn of the Screw*

R

RAMAGE, DR. ROBERT: A little man who moves with a warning air on tiptoe, and has a candid circular face that suggests a large pill. From fussy bewilderment at Julia Bream's death he comes, four years later, to manage with authority and decision the confusion after her daughter Effie's murder, passing it off with unethical competence as the result of a sudden fatal illness. *The Other House*

RANCE, MR.: Forms a merciful barrier to his wife's designs on Adam Verver. Both the Miss Lutches have seen him in the flesh, though when separately questioned their descriptions fail to tally. *The Golden Bowl*

RANCE, MRS.: An American lady from one of the smallest states, who takes advantage of her friends the Miss Lutches introducing her into the Ververs' house to pursue the wealthy widower Adam Verver, although she has a husband 'in un-diminished existence'. *The Golden Bowl*

RANDAGE, OLD: His executors have just come across some 'awful' things in his literary remains. *The Awkward Age*

RANSOM, BASIL: A tall, lean, handsome young Mississippian who has left his impoverished ancient patrimonial estate to practise law in New York and provide for his mother and sisters. Formerly fighting for the South in the Civil War and given to reactionary views on modern society, including the position of women, he does not fit into northern business society, nor can he get his political articles published. Most fatefully he alienates his progressive, touchy Bostonian cousin Olive Chancellor; they compete for dominance over the beautiful, gifted women's rights speaker Verena Tarrant, with whom Basil falls in love. It disgusts him to see her speak in public, and when the luck turns—his article is published—his powerful will and her growing love for him prevail against Olive: he carries her off at the opening of her greatest public lecture to marry her and make her eloquent influence 'truly social' by employing it only in their home circle. His southern chivalry in social circles is matched by autocratic inflexibility in important matters, and he intends to protect and control his independent bride. *The Bostonians*

RANSOM, MRS.: Mother of Basil Ransom, remaining with her daughters on the formerly slave-owning plantation ruined in the Civil War. *The Bostonians*

RINGROSE, LADY: A lady of 'fast' reputation, and so a com-promising friend to Selina Berrington, whose husband will not permit her to enter his house. She surprises Selina's sister Laura Wing by appearing eventually as a well-read lady with short hair and a monocle. She assists in Selina's later elopement. *A London Life*

ROBINSON, HYACINTH: Illegitimate child of Florentine Vivier and her lover Lord Frederick Purvis, whom she kills. Hyacinth is marked permanently as a sensitive child by discovering his mother's crime, and his career reflects his mixed inheritance from the 'passionate plebeian mother' and his 'supercivilised sire'. Brought up by Florentine's dressmaker friend Miss Pynsent, he becomes a clever, slightly built, still sensitive young man of delicate appearance, and learns to be a skilled and artistic bookbinder. Fellow-feeling for the underprivileged predisposes him to revolutionism, and his friend Paul Muniment involves him eventually in an assassination plot. Meanwhile, however, the beautiful, fascinating Princess Casamassima cultivates him for his social views, but paradoxically her beauty and culture begin to convert those views to admiring conservatism. Naturally this undermines his assassinatory enthusiasm, and his mental conflict grows as his friends, caught up in their own affairs, neglect him: even Millicent Henning, his robust, affectionate childhood sweetheart, follows the lure of money and social glamour. His diverse allegiances spring from his complex character and background, and he at last escapes his dilemma by suicide. *The Princess Casamassima*

ROCHEFIDÈLE, COMTE DE LA: An antique gentleman with a wig and profuse white neckcloth in the fashion of 1820: his old age is 'as rosy and round and polished as an imitation apple'. He is polite to the American Newman. *The American*

ROCHEFIDÈLE, COMTESSE DE LA: An old lady in red satin and an ermine cape, whose ancient, cadaverous face is afflicted with a falling of the lower jaw that makes her speech unintelligible to strangers. Her presentation to the American Newman is intended as a great honour to him. *The American*

ROKER: *see* Grugan, Roker and Hotchkin

ROOTH, MIRIAM: A young woman of possibly genteel and certainly Bohemian background, whose dedication to becoming a great actress is stronger than her mother's more social ambitions. Initially awkward with mere hints of talent, she shamelessly badgers a celebrated actress for guidance and influential people for support. She practises indefatigably and progresses amazingly. Her early mentor Peter Sherringham, falling in love with her, cannot understand why she will not leave the stage to become his wife—of course he cannot marry a working actress, or leave his own diplomatic career—but she, without even considering this, marries her colleague and manager Basil Dashwood, who will be suitably devoted to her career. Though her own profession absorbs her, she spares neither others nor herself in pursuing perfection, and apart from this seems to have no definable character under the many she assumes. *The Tragic Muse*

ROOTH, MRS.: An old lady with a shawl—an old voluminous cashmere garment which she characteristically and constantly trails down and hitches up. Widow of Jewish stockbroker Rudoph Roth she claims to have been a Neville-Nugent of Castle Nugent, and insulates herself from her sordid, penurious life by plunging into an endless series of bad novels. *The Tragic Muse*

ROTH, RUDOLPH: Miriam Rooth's father, a Jewish stockbroker and trader in *objets d'art*: he is said to have eloped with Miss Neville-Nugent after giving her piano lessons. Dies young before he has made more than a small fortune. *The Tragic Muse*

ROSENHEIM, MR. AND MRS. D. S., MISS CORA AND MASTER SAMUEL: The news that they and visitors like them have 'left for Brussels' is studied solemnly by Delia Dosson, though she does not know them. Francie Dosson does not care. *The Reverberator*

ROSIER, EDWARD: Acquainted in childhood with Isabel Archer, who remembers him as an angelic little boy who is forbidden by his nursemaid to go to the edge of the lake. Growing up into a very gentle and gracious youth, who sees Paris and indeed life in terms of his precious collection of antiques and bibelots, he still safely 'never goes to the edge of the lake' until he meets the equally charming and innocent Pansy Osmond. Then he makes the supreme sacrifice of his collection to amass money enough for her hostile father—in vain, for like Pansy, his gentleness makes him an unconsidered victim in the plans of more ruthless people. *The Portrait of a Lady*

ROSIER, MR.: Rescues the young Archer sisters when they are abandoned in France by their eloping nursemaid. *The Portrait of a Lady*

ROSSITERS, THE: Their house in New York has an elegant conservatory and seems to Mrs. Ludlow just the thing for her newly enriched sister Isabel Archer. *The Portrait of a Lady*

ROVER, MISS FANNY: A pretty, quick, clever, comic actress, whose friendship with Miriam Rooth represents the raffish, Bohemian area of her life. *The Tragic Muse*

ROWLAND, CAPTAIN: Grandfather of Rowland Mallet, a sea-captain who retires on his savings from some private tradings. Evidently bored, he makes one last voyage, returning mysteriously with a large, placid Dutch bride. *Roderick Hudson*

ROWLAND, MRS.: A handsome, fair woman from Amsterdam brought back to America by Captain Rowland. Does her hair in fantastically elaborate plaits. A tranquil neighbour and excellent housewife, she is homesick, and retiring: her stoutness is later increased by dropsy. *Roderick Hudson*

RUFFLER, MRS.: An actress in the play during which Hyacinth Robinson first meets Princess Casamassima. *The Princess Cassamassima*
References to her form part of Dashwood's and Miriam Rooth's talking 'shop'. *The Tragic Muse*

RUGGIERI, SIGNOR: An Italian tragedian in Rome who has taught Miriam Rooth to pronounce Italian and to declaim and gesticulate (too much). *The Tragic Muse*

RYE, LORD: One of the clients for whom Mrs. Jordan does the flower arrangements. She hints, in gossip, that he is romantically interested in her. *In the Cage*

S

SAINT DUNSTANS, LADY: A very old lady, godmother of Sir Nicholas Dormer, with whom his widow Lady Agnes and her daughter Grace go to stay. *The Tragic Muse*

SAINT DUNSTANS, LORD: An English Catholic peer, the father of the elder Marquise de Bellegarde. *The American*

SAINTONGE, MLLE. DE: Among the guests of Mme. de Brécourt whose brother Gaston Probert prefers to dine with the newly-met Dossons. *The Reverberator*

SANDERS, MRS.: An American lady from Boston who recommends a tutor for young Randolph Miller in Europe. *Daisy Miller*

SANDS, MISS: A New York beauty accustomed to social triumph, in whom Roger Lawrence shows interest, but only because she resembles his ward Nora Lambert. Miss Sands' growing preference for him is in vain. *Watch and Ward*

SAVAGE, MISS: *see* Light, Mrs.

SAVAGE, MR.: An old American painter of bad landscapes, a mild, melancholy, pitiful gentleman, ill-treated by his actress wife, who sells his pictures. His daughter Mrs. Light returns to him as a widow but to escape her own creditors leaves him again infirm and starving. A subscription is raised to send him back to America where he dies. *Roderick Hudson*

SAVAGE, MRS.: A dreadful English actress, who ill-treats her husband and uses her beauty to sell his bad paintings. Eventually elopes with an English lord. *Roderick Hudson*

SCHAAFGANS, HERR: A German artist of spiritual leanings and eccentric mediaeval dress, whose paintings are extremely angular. Marries his Roman model, is ruined, beaten by his wife and takes to drink. Mme. Grandoni tells his story to Roderick Hudson as a warning against extremes of aspiration and recklessness. *Roderick Hudson*

SCHACK, OR SCHMACK, BARON: A very rich Jew, who has a stammer or no roof to his mouth, and hires Algie Manger to 'do his conversation for him', a job coveted by Harold Brookenham. *The Awkward Age*

SCHINKEL: A German cabinet maker with a long, unhealthy, benevolent face, greasy hair and an untidy bandage round his neck, like a very tame horse whose collar galls him. A member of the anarchist group that includes Paul Muniment and Hyacinth Robinson, he is discreet, pedantic and reliable, and is entrusted to deliver to Hyacinth the sealed instructions for an assassination attempt. He watches Hyacinth's room thereafter in vague foreboding, justified by Hyacinth's suicide. *The Princess Casamassima*

SCHOOLING, MISS FANNY AND MISS KATIE: Described at great length by Mr. Wendover to Laura Wing, who hardly knows them, perhaps because he has no other topic of conversation ready. *A London Life*

SCHOOLING, MRS. FANNY: Writes an introductory letter for Mr. Wendover to Selina Berrington, whom she admires. (Selina thinks her incurably provincial.) *A London Life*

SCUDAMORE, R. P.: A typical American name as seen on luggage in the Dossons' Parisian hotel. *The Reverberator*

SERVER, MRS. MAY: A beautiful society woman with auburn hair, who often has her portrait painted. She crowns an unfortunate life—an unpleasant husband, the death of her children—with a love affair with the handsome, dull Gilbert Long, changing him into a perceptive, clever man, but losing all her own brilliance in the process. Exhausted, she tries with conspicuous and unsuccessful activity to appear her former bright heart-whole self, but lapses into weariness as Long is now turning to the clever, pretty, rejuvenated Grace Brissenden. *The Sacred Fount*

SHEPHERD, SUSAN: *see* Stringham, Mrs. Susan Shepherd

SHERRINGHAM, PETER: A young diplomat with a foreign-looking brown complexion, pointed beard and lively expression overlying his basic Englishness. A lifelong friend, neighbour and second cousin of the Dormers, he is loved by Biddy Dormer but falls in love with actress Miriam Rooth. He admires dramatic art, but ultimately considers it as necessarily less important than the world of diplomacy. Therefore he demands that Miriam leave the stage to marry him and use her talent in diplomatic circles. She, however, is like Nick Dormer in valuing the arts above public affairs, and instead of becoming a diplomat's wife, suggests he become an actress's husband. Outraged, he spends a year in South America, but returns prepared to compromise—too late, for she has just married her manager, Dashwood. He is consoled gradually by recognising the dramatic greatness that justifies her dedication, and eventually marries Biddy. *The Tragic Muse*

SHOLTO, CAPTAIN GODFREY: The occasionally tolerated admirer of Princess Casamassima. A curious and not particularly edifying English type, his 'longish pedigree' and moderate income make him a gentleman of unmitigated leisure, without talents or tastes to distinguish him, and the Princess regards his hopeless passion for herself as attitudinising to occupy his time. He takes her advice to cultivate other women, and achieves some success with Millicent Henning; this is unfortunate for Hyacinth Robinson who, desperately seeking comfort before his suicide, sees even the wholesome Millicent, his childhood sweetheart, as tainted by Sholto's social and economic influence. *The Princess Casamassima*

SILBERSTADT-SCHRECKENSTEIN, PRINCE ADOLF OF: Morganatically married to Eugenia Münster. Though a 'ninny', he retains some attachment to her in spite of their separation, and Eugenia plays on this to strengthen her position when their marriage is threatened with dissolution. *The Europeans*

SILBERSTADT-SCHRECKENSTEIN, REIGNING PRINCE OF: A clever man, he plans a political marriage for his younger brother Adolf, whose morganatic marriage to Eugenia Münster he therefore wishes to dissolve. Though absolute in his power, he has promised not to act without Eugenia's consent. *The Europeans*

SIMPKIN'S, LADLE'S AND THRUPP'S: Names of high-class blocks of apartments in Mayfair whose inhabitants patronise Crocker's shop. *In the Cage*

SINGLETON, SAM: A small American artist of great modesty, who looks like a precocious child. A water-colourist whose early unpromising daubs have been improved by patient industry to reveal a slender and delicate but incontestable talent. His perseverance and dedication, as much as his uncritical admiration of Roderick Hudson, become an ironic reflection on Roderick's later deterioration, weakness and temper. Sam returns to his family in Buffalo, New York, regretfully but with a portfolio of nine hundred sketches. *Roderick Hudson*

SLOPER, DR. AUSTIN: A clever man and a good doctor, who balances scholarly knowledge with conspicuous practical skill. His vocation is made easier by his marriage to a rich and beautiful woman. However for all his skill his promising infant son and his wife both die, and his surviving baby daughter Catherine grows up to be a robust but dull girl. Disappointed, he fulfils his duty by forbidding her marriage to fortune-hunter Morris Townsend, but has no sympathy for her feelings. Taking her to Europe to forget Morris he admits that he himself is not a good man; his firmness and self-assurance cause him to leave Catherine, by then a middle-aged old maid, a reduced inheritance because she will not humiliate herself by promising never to marry the long departed Morris. Duty and restraint are virtues he possesses, but real goodness, as he says—mercy, self-denial, generosity—is foreign to him. *Washington Square*

SLOPER, MRS. CATHERINE: Née Harrington. A very charming, amiable, graceful, accomplished New York girl who is also very rich. She marries the young Austin Sloper, who is poor but already distinguished and 'promising'. Loses her little son, then dies herself a week after giving birth to Catherine. *Washington Square*

SLOPER, CATHERINE: A robust girl who disappoints her clever father Dr. Sloper for, though affectionate, docile and kind, both her face and intellect are plain, gentle and dull. Unromantic by nature, at twenty-one she admires her father with love touched by fear, so that when handsome, penniless Morris Townsend becomes her first suitor, her father's implacable opposition makes her suffer, and she defies him doggedly rather than passionately. Discouraged by Dr. Sloper's determination to disinherit her, and dissatisfied by her own modest fortune, Morris jilts her. Disillusioned not only by Morris but by her father's coldness, she refuses two further suitors and becomes a staid old maid whose appearance of active contentment is her form of dignity. Eventually her stubborn self-respect defeats both the men who have humiliated her—she refuses her father the satisfaction of a promise never to marry Morris, and refuses even a token friendship to the returning, older, still unsuccessful Morris himself. *Washington Square*

SMALLSHAW, MR.: Lionel Berrington's clever lawyer. *A London Life*

SPOONER, MR.: A lawyer, partner of Mr. Striker and co-employer of Roderick Hudson. *Roderick Hudson*

STACKPOLE, HENRIETTA: A neat, plump person with round face, small mouth, light brown ringlets and peculiarly open, surprised-looking eyes that shine with great clarity and fix the world without embarrassment. A well-known journalist in America, she visits England partly professionally, partly to see her friend Isabel Archer whose European contacts she disapproves of, considering everything American superior to everything European. Particularly (and rightly) disapproving of Isabel's husband Gilbert Osmond, she later returns again to try to help Isabel in her unhappiness. Her directness, boldness and independence suggest blatant immodesty to Osmond, but in fact are based on what she has in common with Isabel, the shining, essential honesty of the American girl. Finally she gives up independence to marry her English friend and frequent fellow traveller Bob Bantling, a romantic step which both feel to be less a banal conclusion of their comradeship than a plunge into the unknown. *The Portrait of a Lady*

STAMM, LISA: While young and beautiful she is abandoned by her betrothed and takes refuge in the Roman Sepolte Vive convent, where no word of the inmates is ever given. Her sister Mlle. Stamm has come to Rome for her sake. *Watch and Ward*

STAMM, MLLE.: An old German lady, a queer wizened oddity of a woman, whose young beautiful sister Lisa long ago took refuge in a Roman convent of particular strictness. She leaves flowers there for Lisa but cannot know whether her sister is dead or alive. A philosopher perforce, she befriends Nora Lambert. *Watch and Ward*

STANT, CHARLOTTE: A tall, strong, charming girl whose unusual narrow face, large mouth and tawny brown hair make her unexpectedly beautiful. Her poverty prevents her marrying debt-ridden Prince Amerigo, and she leaves precipitately for her native but hated America. Meanwhile he becomes engaged to her rich, gentle friend Maggie Verver. Charlotte arrives suddenly in England, ostensibly to buy a wedding present, actually to testify to her continuing love for Amerigo. (And while considering as a present a Golden Bowl with a hidden crack she hints at a future liaison: the Prince honourably rejects both the bowl and the suggestion.) After hesitating, Charlotte agrees to marry Maggie's widowed father

Adam. Both she and the Prince begin with good intentions but, exasperated by their spouses' complacent withdrawal into habitual domesticity, they decide merely to hide hurtful evidence of their belated love affair. Charlotte covertly demands tolerance from the eventually suspicious Maggie, for Adam's sake, but she underestimates her husband: he not only has perceived the whole situation but acts decisively, taking the dangerous Charlotte back to America. Charlotte suffers secretly, especially as the Prince has come to prefer Maggie, but claims that her exile is her own plan to remove Adam from his possessive daughter. Maggie compassionately accepts this role, and thus Charlotte's assumption of a dignified position augurs well for her new start with Adam. *The Golden Bowl*

STEET, MISS: The martyred-looking nursery governess of the little Berringtons. The daughter of a clergyman, she is discouraged by her employers' indifference to her pupils and their progress, but as this is all she has to complain of, her pupils' aunt, Laura Wing, feels sometimes exasperated by her perpetual melancholy. However in the emergency of Mrs. Berrington's elopement she willingly helps Laura set off to appeal to her sister. *A London Life*

STOCK-STOCK, MRS.: An English friend whom the Misses Bordereau have loved dearly: she is dead and gone, poor dear. *The Aspern Papers*

STRETHER, LEWIS LAMBERT: An American of five-and-fifty, with brown face, thick dark moustache, thick greying hair and a nose of bold free prominence—he always wears glasses. From lack of opportunity or opportunism he has failed in every relationship and half a dozen trades, leaving him with not a crowded experience but memories of 'dreadful, cheerful, sociable solitude'. Therefore when he arrives in Paris and is struck with its charm and all the joy of life he has missed, his advice to a young friend is, positively, 'Live!' Mrs. Newsome, not only his fiancée but also, as owner of the review he edits, his employer, has sent him to Paris to reclaim her son Chad from rumoured entanglement with a Parisienne. Amazed however by Chad's new grace, polish and sophistication, and later charmed by the married Mme. de Vionnet who has transformed Chad, Strether ends by opposing rather than encouraging Chad's offer to leave her. Though Mrs. Newsome withdraws her confidence and, sending her married daughter Sarah Pocock for a more reliable opinion, remains sure that no social polish can excuse immoral relationships, Strether remains converted to Parisian values of living life to the full. None the less, to prove his conversion is a considered one and not mere laxity, he decides to return to argue with Mrs. Newsome instead of remaining to develop his own relationship with his devoted confidante, Maria Gostrey. *The Ambassadors*

STRETHER, MRS.: Young wife of Lambert Strether, who dies early. He reproaches himself with mourning her death so much that he neglects their dull little son, who dies of rapid diphtheria while away at school. *The Ambassadors*

STRETT, SIR LUKE: A very famous London doctor, who with his large, settled face looks half like a general, half like a bishop. Consulted by Milly Theale, he tells her only that she must live and do as she likes—which she correctly interprets as meaning she must make the most of her remaining time. His long visits to her in Venice indicate the desperation of her case (and the immensity of her fortune). *The Wings of the Dove*

STRIKER, MR. BARNABY: A lean, sandy-haired solicitor, who employs Roderick Hudson as a clerk and has a low opinion of him. Shrewd and good-natured, he makes the prophetic warning that in turning to sculpture Roderick will need determination and persistence as well as inspiration. *Roderick Hudson*

STRIKER, MRS.: Is invited to Roderick Hudson's farewell picnic party, but does not come. *Roderick Hudson*

STRIKER, PETRONILLA: Daughter of the Strikers, a young lady with pale blue eyes, who comes to Roderick Hudson's farewell picnic party, dressed as if to sit for her photograph, though a bit of a romp. Sits for a long time by the lake with Roderick. *Roderick Hudson*

STRINGHAM, MRS. SUSAN SHEPHERD: A small, elderly Boston lady, who, having lost husband and mother and being child-less, lives 'sharply single' on her small income, writing short stories for the best magazines, aimed at the non-domestic literary woman. Intrigued by the striking, unusual heiress Milly Theale, she is thrilled to be invited to travel in Europe with her. It is her own old schoolfellow Maud Lowder who introduces them successfully into London society and provides a friend for Milly, her own niece Kate Croy. Quaint with 'the new quaintness', Susan bores Kate but has immeasurable powers of perception about her adored Milly. She has guessed Milly's incurable illness, and connives in the attentions of Kate's fiancé Merton Densher, in the hopes that he may make her happy or even save her. However, she is generous enough to realise his passive benevolence cannot extend to denying outright his secret engagement to Kate, and she bears no resentment when Milly, learning the truth, despairs and dies. *The Wings of the Dove*

STURTEVANT, MISS: Her attractions are obvious to the dullest comprehension and John Ludlow marries her after unsuccessfully and inexplicably falling in love with the plain, dull Catherine Sloper. *Washington Square*

T

TACCHINI, DR.: The Italian doctor nominally attending Milly Theale in Venice between Sir Luke Strett's visits, but though he is proud of Sir Luke's coaching Milly will not actually see him. *The Wings of the Dove*

TANTRUM, LORD AND LADY: Among the guests of Mme. de Brécourt whose brother Gaston Probert prefers to dine with the newly-met Dossons. *The Reverberator*

TARRANT, DR. SELAH: Verena's father, a mesmeric healer who begins life as an itinerant vendor of pencils, is a member of the celebrated Cayuga community (where matrimony is eccentrically observed) and later leads his wife and daughter an unsettled life of cranky movements and reforms. Nevertheless he has the sublime quality of never admitting, however privately, to any failure or deceit. An unsuccessful public speaker, disappointed in his ambition to figure in the newspapers, he takes vicarious satisfaction in the success of his daughter who is unlike him in eloquence, celebrity and honesty. *The Bostonians*

TARRANT, MRS.: Daughter of the celebrated Abolitionist Abraham Greenstreet, she marries beneath her, choosing the mesmerist and faith healer Selah Tarrant, whom she comes both to admire and despise. A white, puffy woman who still clings to a mythical social position, she pushes her daughter Verena into friendship with rich, distinguished Olive Chancellor, and never ceases her attempts to intrude into their circle herself. *The Bostonians*

TARRANT, VERENA: A beautiful young woman with red hair who in spite of being the daughter of the hypocritical quack healer has retained absolute naturalness, spontaneity and honesty. Her remarkable, irresistible but mysterious talent for extemporised public speaking and her flexible intelligence are harnessed to her interest in women's emancipation, but her essential character is not assertive but completely and generously responsive to others. Thus, dominated at first by her friend Olive Chancellor, Verena is absorbed in the women's rights campaign that Olive also cares for, but her sympathy and growing love for the reactionary Basil Ransom begins to conflict with her innate talents, of which he disapproves. Finally her love for Basil wins, and she abandons Olive and her greatest public meeting to marry him, departing in tears which are 'not the last she was destined to shed.' Though her great responsiveness no doubt inspires her eloquence, it also confuses her, and her many-sidedness means that she renounces much happiness if she has to choose only one. *The Bostonians*

TATTON, MR.: The Brookenham's butler. *The Awkward Age*

TELEGRAPHIST, THE: A young woman whose family have long descended from original gentility (her mother now drinks). She works in a general Post Office in Mayfair where her duties of sending telegrams and her romantic imagination involve her in the drama of handsome Captain Everard, a regular customer, whose secret but well telegrammed affair with Lady Bradeen she follows; her imagination is so filled with this that she delays marriage to her fiancé the stolid Mr. Mudge. Scrupulously avoiding any repetition of her one personal encounter with Everard, she saves him from scandal by recalling verbatim the terms of a compromising telegram. When she learns that his love for the newly widowed Lady Bradeen has waned with the necessity of marrying her, the Telegraphist prudently decides to prevent her fantasy life becoming too real by marrying Mudge quickly and moving away. *In the Cage*

TERESITA (TERESA): A young Spanish lady of Peru with whom Roger Lawrence becomes infatuated. Her charm lies less in her liquid hazel eyes and blue-black hair than in her naïve, unspoilt (indeed almost illiterate) manner. At first preferring her simplicity to his ward's painstaking education, Roger changes his mind and leaves Peru. She later makes an excellent match to a young merchant of Valparaiso. *Watch and Ward*

THEALE, MILLY: A young American girl, whose beauty is arguable: she is 'constantly pale, delicately haggard, anomalously, agreeably angular', and has hair 'somehow exceptionally red even for the real thing'. Only survivor of the successive tragic deaths of her whole family, she is now very rich but something prompts her to travel through Europe (with her older Boston friend Susan Stringham) increasingly hastily *en route* to consult an eminent doctor in London. Rightly interpreting his comment that she is well and must live to the full, as meaning that she will get worse and should make the most of her short span, she falls in love with Merton Densher. This is threatened by his secret engagement to her friend Kate Croy, but Kate and he pretend that his suit is unsuccessful, partly to help Milly, partly to deceive Kate's hostile rich aunt, and partly in hopes that Milly will enrich Densher, even if he has to marry her. But a suitor of both girls, Lord Mark, guesses their interest in Densher, and betrays the deception to Milly, thus turning her new will to live to despair and death. Generously appreciating Densher's motives, however, she leaves him an enormous fortune. Too late he reacts against Kate's ruthless courage and loves Milly's memory. Dove-like in her innocence, Milly also has great strength: her unselfishness cannot save herself but perhaps saves Densher's self-respect. *The Wings of the Dove*

THOMPSON, MR., AND FANE, MRS.: Typical imaginary names used by children playing at being grown-ups, an impression created by the innocent Mr. Verver and his daughter Maggie. *The Golden Bowl*

THRUPP'S: *see* Simpkin's, Ladle's and Thrupp's

TISCHBEIN, MR.: An admirer of Ida Farange who offers to take her to South Africa, whereupon she formally hands over her daughter Maisie to her estranged second husband Sir Claude. *What Maisie Knew*

TOOVEY, MR.: A man 'in the City'. Marries Vanderbank's sister. *The Awkward Age*

TOOVEY, NANCY: Born Blanche Bertha Vanderbank. Her transition to this new name in her married state bewilders Mr. Longdon, who knew her as a girl. *The Awkward Age*

TOPPING, MISS: Calls herself Florine or Dorine. A source of Parisian scandal used by George Flack, she has supplied rumours to eke out the gossip he gleaned from Francie Dosson about the Proberts. *The Reverberator*

TOUCHETT, MR. DANIEL TRACY: An old American banker, long domiciled in England where he preserves intact his American physiognomy—narrow, clean-shaven face, features evenly distributed, expression of placid acuteness. With all his deep experience of mankind he retains an almost rustic simplicity on some subjects, and there are depths and obscurities he is the better for never plumbing. Regretful over the usual absence of his eccentric wife, he provides the more maternal influence on their son Ralph, supplying also the example of his own generosity, tolerance, honesty and contemplative intelligence. He is persuaded by Ralph to leave a large fortune to his wife's niece Isabel Archer, about which he rightly has misgivings. *The Portrait of a Lady*

TOUCHETT, MRS. LYDIA: A plain-faced old woman without graces and without any real elegance, but with great force of personality, very fond of her own way, which she pursues with rational imperturbability, her motives usually being quite different from what observers suppose. Her incompatibility with her husband is not concealed but institutionalised by her living consistently in Florence and visiting him at set intervals. During a visit to her native America she takes up her niece Isabel Archer, and by introducing her to Europe and her friend Mme. Merle she unwittingly precipitates Isabel's unhappy marriage to Mme. Merle's friend Gilbert Osmond. Unlike Mme. Merle, Mrs. Touchett is absolutely honest and straightforward, but her prosaic lack of emotional ties, memories and even regrets, threaten her with a bleak old age, as her husband and son predecease her. *The Portrait of a Lady*

TOUCHETT, RALPH: Son of the Touchetts, well-educated in England and America, but his career in banking is cut short when a neglected cold affects his lungs—he has to spend his winters in hot countries but still steadily deteriorates. Condemned to be an onlooker in life he shows his love for his cousin Isabel Archer by persuading his father to bequeath half his own legacy to her, but his remorse is great when the money only attracts the mercenary Gilbert Osmond, and his attempt to prevent their marriage loses him Isabel's confidence. However she comes to share his judgement of Gilbert's egotistic dilettantism, and defying her husband returns from Italy to Ralph's deathbed to confess this. His generosity and tolerance is innate rather than an invalid's detachment, and where Isabel is concerned he is deeply involved whether he intends it or not. *The Portrait of a Lady*

TOWNSEND, ARTHUR: A little stockbroker, engaged and later married to Marian Almond. Very practical and unimaginative himself, he considers his cousin Morris Townsend 'too clever' and conceited, but is the means of introducing him to Marian's cousin Catherine Sloper. *Washington Square*

TOWNSEND, MORRIS: A tall, handsome young man with delicate, chiselled, finished features, who has spent his small fortune and lives on his poor widowed sister Mrs. Montgomery. He wins the affection of plain, dull, but rich Catherine Sloper, but decides her personal fortune is too small and as her father, who dislikes him, will not leave her more money if they marry, Morris jilts her. Twenty years later, widowed and poor, he returns from Europe, still handsome though with thinning hair and thickening figure, to approach Catherine again, but in vain: she is no longer to be charmed. *Washington Square*

TRESSILIAN, FLORENCE: A tremendously nice, clever, old and safe friend of Biddy Dormer. Moves into that great novelty, a flat, with all kinds of lifts and tubes and electricities. An enlightened modern spinster. *The Tragic Muse*

TRISTRAM, MRS. LIZZIE: Wife of Tom Tristram, she has a very plain face and considerable intelligence, and is a strange mixture of timidity and restlessness, avid imagination and personal reserve. Encourages her husband's friend Newman to fall in love with her own friend Claire de Cintré, and sympathises and understands when Claire's family forbid the match. *The American*

TRISTRAM, TOM: A pleasant, idle, American friend of Christopher Newman; lives in Paris. He is large, smooth and pink, with the air of a successfully potted plant. Unable to understand deep feelings, he advises Newman against falling in love with Claire de Cintré and regards him as well out of it when she is separated from him. *The American*

TUCKER, MRS.: An American known to Ida Farange, not of noble rank like Beale Farange's 'Countess'. *What Maisie Knew*

U

UPJOHN, MISS KITTY: An American in Paris, a friend of the Tristrams. *The American*

V

VAN: *see* Vanderbank, Gustavus

VANDERBANK, GUSTAVUS (VAN): A very handsome, pleasant, charming young man, one of Mrs. Brookenham's witty, frivolous, gossiping social circle. Although his flippant modernity amazes Mr. Longdon, a rich, elderly, retiring friend of his mother's, he is not totally frivolous: he holds to certain values. Instead of perceiving the virtues of emancipation in Nanda Brookenham who loves him, these values make him conventionally shocked at her frankness and imprudence, and not even Mr. Longdon's promise of a large settlement of money can make him marry her (though certainly Mrs. Brookenham, who wants him to herself, is also responsible for applying some very clever pressure against his ever marrying). Well meaning and sincere, he cannot help his double standard, and probably returns to a comparatively conventional illicit relationship with Mrs. Brookenham. *The Awkward Age*

VANDERBANK, MARY: Vanderbank's sister, recollected by Mr. Longdon but now long dead. *The Awkward Age*

VANDERBANK, MILES: Vanderbank's brother, very clever and promising, but of frail health, who dies at seventeen. *The Awkward Age*

VARIAN, MISS: A cousin of Isabel Archer. Her half-dozen bedside paperbacked novels are the only books in her mother's expensive house. *The Portrait of a Lady*

VARIAN, MRS.: Paternal aunt of Isabel Archer, who falsely supposes her niece to be writing a book. She has a theoretic reverence for literature, although, bringing up her daughters 'properly', she avoids controversy by allowing them to read nothing at all. *The Portrait of a Lady*

VAVASOUR, MAUD; EDITH TEMPLE; GLADYS VANE: Euphonious stage names invented by Miriam Rooth. She eventually decides to keep her own real name. *The Tragic Muse*

VENTNOR, LADY: One of the clients for whom Mrs. Jordan does flower arrangements. *In the Cage*

VERNEUIL, MARIE: Celebrated French women's rights militant, released from prison only a few weeks before Olive Chancellor and Verena Tarrant visit her. *The Bostonians*

VERVER, ADAM: Fabulously rich widowed American industrialist, unobtrusive in appearance but for very striking, deep blue changeful eyes, whose passion for his 'interests' is later superseded by a passion and taste for beautiful antiquities and *objets d'art*: he is building up a priceless collection for his museum in American City. These passions however are always secondary to his love for Maggie, his daughter and devoted companion since her childhood. After her marriage to Prince Amerigo, seeing her perpetual worry about him, he decides to marry her girlhood friend Charlotte Stant. This results not in his devotion to Charlotte, but to his and Maggie's resumption of their old companionship, leaving the Prince and Charlotte together, dangerously, as the latter two were once secretly in love. Alerted by Maggie's eventual uneasiness, Adam shows himself less vulnerable in his gentle honesty than the others imagine. Decisively and inexorably he takes Charlotte back to America, which she hates, away from his beloved daughter, ruthless to himself and his wife in protecting Maggie's happiness. His amiability, which many take advantage of, seems inconsistent with his financial exploits, until his underlying force is revealed: 'he knew coldly, quite bleakly, where he would, at the crisis, draw the line', and his honesty, integrity and sensitivity do not therefore make him a victim of the less scrupulous. *The Golden Bowl*

VERVER, MAGGIE: A slight, pretty, almost nun-like girl, heiress of Adam Verver. After growing up as her devoted father's companion she marries Prince Amerigo, not knowing he has just broken off a hopeless love affair with her friend Charlotte Stant. Ironically then, still concerned for her father's loneliness, Maggie welcomes his marriage to the young, penniless but beautiful and clever Charlotte. This solution somehow results in her spending more time with her father, throwing Charlotte and the Prince much together, but eventually Maggie realises her danger. Believing at first that she can prevent an incipient affair, she learns, by buying a Golden Bowl from a man who remembers Charlotte and the Prince nearly buying it together, of their old-established relationship. Her bitterness is alleviated by a sense of the Prince's new appreciation of her; this, and concern for her father, make her apparently submit to Charlotte's veiled demands for complacency. Encouraged by gaining the Prince's allegiance from Charlotte, and effectively saved by her father's ruthless decision to take Charlotte to America, she accepts the pretence that Charlotte wishes to have Adam to herself, thus launching her in a more dignified role, though at her expense. Maggie's powers of self-control grow as her experience widens, and though remaining sweet and gentle she becomes more mature. *The Golden Bowl*

VERVER, MRS.: Adam Verver's very young first wife, whose first trip with him to Paris is notable for her buying lots of ugly fashionable clothes: he wonders later whether her taste would have affected his or his hers. *The Golden Bowl*

VERVER, MRS. CHARLOTTE: *see* Stant, Charlotte

VETCH, ANASTASIUS: An elderly violinist in a second-rate theatre orchestra, friend and neighbour of Miss Pynsent. Though warning her that any choice she makes will be held against her, he advises her to take her protégé Hyacinth Robinson to his mother's deathbed in prison, rather than conceal his criminal origins from him. Feeling therefore some responsibility as well as affection for Hyacinth, he finds him work as a craftsman bookbinder. His own origins seem to be in a higher social sphere but he has become a 'lonely, disappointed, embittered, cynical little man'. However his destructive social attitude not only mellows with age but is rejected in his concern at Hyacinth's more actively destructive revolutionary involvement: guessing his dangerous assassinatory mission, he intervenes in vain, unless his pleas and arguments increase the confusion that ends in Hyacinth's suicide. *The Princess Casamassima*

VETCH, FLEDA: An intelligent, sensitive and discriminating girl. Without money or artistic background, except a year's training in a Paris studio, she becomes confidante of the connoisseur Mrs. Gereth, whose priceless collection of treasures in her former home Poynton are all bequeathed by her late husband to their son Owen. Acting as intermediary between mother and son after Mrs. Gereth has carried off too many of her former 'things' from Poynton, Fleda is torn between sympathy for her and her own growing love for Owen. Embarrassed, Fleda avoids him until, disgusted by his fiancée Mona Brigstock's demands for the return of the 'spoils', he seeks out Fleda to propose marriage. Scrupulously she sends him back to break formally with Mona, but she underestimates his weakness and Mona's ruthlessness, for the next she hears is that Mona has peremptorily married him. Grief stricken, Fleda devotes herself to the bereft but generous Mrs. Gereth, and Owen's later offer of her choice of Poynton's treasures results in her witnessing the virtual destruction of Poynton by fire: the lives of everyone except Mona are now as diminished as the treasures are. *The Spoils of Poynton*

VETCH, MAGGIE: Sister of Fleda, she marries a curate whose

elder brother is said to have money; however, they live in a mean little house in a stupid little town, possessed of scant mahogany furniture. *The Spoils of Poynton*

VETCH, MR.: Father of Fleda and Maggie, tolerates rather than welcomes Fleda's presence, doddering off to his club as if he were seventy instead of fifty-seven, returning only at midnight. He pities Fleda's lack of appreciation of his collection of gimcracks, unaware of her love for the priceless treasures of Poynton. *The Spoils of Poynton*

VIDAL, DENNIS: A short, meagre young man with smooth face and dark blue sailor jacket, all of which (including the jacket) seem only intensified when he returns a second time from China, still fascinated by Rose Armiger, who jilted him four years earlier. Her apparent willingness to accept him again shows her despair as Tony Bream whom she loves obviously prefers her rival Jean Martle. When in a final insane effort she murders Tony's child Effie, hoping to incriminate Jean, Dennis takes her away, his fascination now changed to loathing. *The Other House*

VILLEPREUX, MME. LEONIE DE: Daughter of Mme. de Marignac but not as nice as her mother: brought up with the young Probert girls she later 'carries on' with Maxime de Cliché, the husband of one of them; the scandal is reported in the *Reverberator*. *The Reverberator*

VIONNET, COMTE DE: A high, distinguished, polished, impertinent reprobate. Marries his wife probably for her dowry; they separate and he is such an obviously impossible brute that no one can blame anyone but him. In the marriage of his daughter Jeanne he will take no trouble apart from suggesting half a dozen impossible things. *The Ambassadors*

VIONNET, JEANNE DE: Marriageable but still very young daughter of Mme. de Vionnet. Strether at first wonders whether she is keeping Chad Newsome in Paris but this red herring conceals Chad's love affair with her mother, though she herself is possibly in love with him. Later betrothed to M. de Montbron, her real feelings are never revealed. *The Ambassadors*

VIONNET, MME. DE (MARIE): Beautiful and still youthful though mother of a débutante daughter. Formerly a sensitive, audacious child of nature she is married straight from school to the unsavoury Comte de Vionnet. Judicially separated from him she settles in Paris to bring up her daughter, but is now a charming, civilised woman of the world, and thus captivates the rough young American Chad Newsome, completely remoulding his manners and taste along Parisian lines. More in love than he, she struggles to keep him against his mother's summons and his own qualms. She and Paris captivate his mother's ambassador Strether, but for all Chad's excellent manners Paris cannot give him—perhaps destroys—an excellent heart, and he will probably leave her for the attraction of the commercial world. *The Ambassadors*

VIVIAN, ANGELA: A beautiful, unusually clever young woman whose unconventiality and love for Bernard Longueville are misunderstood by him as bold flirtatiousness, of which he warns his friend Gordon Wright who wants to marry her; guilt about this confuses his next meeting with her. She however knows nothing of this interference and mutual explanations lead to their engagement. When Gordon reappears, ready to divorce his wife Blanche and regarding this engagement as treachery, Angela diagnoses further misunderstandings, swiftly dispels Gordon's persecution mania, and marries Bernard for a life of well-deserved happiness. *Confidence*

VIVIAN, MRS.: A delicate little gentlewoman with fine dark eyes and a band of silver hair. Originally a Bostonian and very honest, she is also clever and civilised by long experience of travelling in Europe for economic reasons; under her meekly proper appearance she is capable of ironic comment. Her influence on the flirtatious Blanche Evers is not at first effective, though when exercised later it repairs Blanche's marriage to Gordon Wright. Mrs. Vivian has earlier failed to influence her own daughter Angela to marry Gordon, but, an affectionate mother, she is happy in Angela's choice of Bernard Longueville. *Confidence*

VIVIER, FLORENTINE: Hyacinth Robinson's unmarried mother, formerly a dressmaker, lively, pretty and French, possessed of 'personal as distinguished from social brilliance'. When she stabs her lover Lord Frederick Purvis to death and is sentenced to life imprisonment she confides Hyacinth to her friend and fellow worker Miss Pynsent, seeing him only once more nine years later when, terribly aged and changed, she is on her deathbed. *The Princess Casamassima*

VIVIER, HYACINTHE: Father of Florentine Vivier, after whom her illegitimate son is named. A revolutionary watchmaker, he dies on the barricades in Paris, and his republicanism is one element in the very mixed inheritance—or at least, imagination—of his complex grandson. *The Princess Casamassima*

VOISIN, MLLE.: A very celebrated actress, a slim distinguished woman who is the star of the Théâtre Français, and dazzles Miriam Rooth by her consummate *savoir-faire*, on stage and off. *The Tragic Muse*

VOSE, MR.: A fat butcher who has just shaved off his side whiskers. When Roger Lawrence does the same to impress his ward Nora Lambert, he unfortunately reminds her of Mr. Vose. *Watch and Ward*

W

WALKER: The Breams' noiseless butler. *The Other House*

WALKER, MRS.: An American friend of Winterbourne, a very accomplished woman who is shocked at the unconventional boldness of Daisy Miller and after trying to advise her, breaks off their acquaintance. *Daisy Miller*

WARBURTON, LORD: A tall, handsome, fresh-coloured Englishman of about thirty-five, with a lively grey eye, rich chestnut beard and a certain fortunate, brilliant, exceptional look. Though a very large landed proprietor he holds radical views and would like to abolish the aristocracy, though his friends doubt if he would really enjoy obscurity. Falls in love with Isabel Archer who refuses him. After her marriage to Gilbert Osmond he seems to be courting her stepdaughter Pansy, and his eventual retreat probably stems less from sympathy with Pansy's obvious preference for another, than from his own continuing love for Isabel. Later professing to be engaged to Lady Flora or Felicia, he seems still ready to pursue Isabel:

he proves fortunate in everything except the one thing he wants. *The Portrait of a Lady*

WARMINGTON, LADY (EVA): The only one of Lady Aurora Langrish's seven sisters to be married. *The Princess Casamassima*

WARMINGTON, LORD: Married to one of Lady Aurora Langrish's sisters. *The Princess Casamassima*

WATERLOW, CHARLES: A young American artist of great promise, who paints in the Impressionist style. His acquaintance George Flack persuades Francie Dosson to let him paint her. Here Francie first meets her future fiancé Gaston Probert, who is urged later by the tough-minded Waterlow to be a man and defy his family in the quarrel arising over Francie. *The Reverberator*

WATERMOUTH, LADY: An invalid friend of the selfish Selina Berrington, whom Selina is always professing to visit at Weybridge. This amazes Selina's naïve sister Laura Wing, until it appears that these visits are camouflage for Selina's affair with Captain Crispin. *A London Life*

WATERWORTHS, THE: A family known to the Vivians in Europe, whom Blanche Evers does not visit because she dislikes too many women together—'five daughters—all unmarried!' *Confidence*

WAYMARSH: A celebrated, successful American barrister with a large handsome head, large sallow seamed face, a great political brow, thick loose hair and dark fuliginous eyes: he resembles some great American statesman of a primitively simple era. Because of overwork and illness he is travelling in Europe, which he dislikes for its sophistication: he warns his old friend Lambert Strether (who has come to snatch Chad Newsome from Paris but is becoming involved in European sophistication himself) to 'Quit it!' Nicknamed Sitting Bull for his impressive silent disapproval, even Waymarsh at last succumbs to the Parisian atmosphere to the extent of developing a sentimental flirtation with Chad's sister Mrs. Sarah Pocock, and his departure from Paris with Mrs. Pocock's party is less patriarchal than his arrival. *The Ambassadors*

WAYMARSH, MRS.: Marries Waymarsh when he is thirty, but has now been separated from him for fifteen years. Lives in

European hotels, paints her face and writes her husband abusive letters. *The Ambassadors*

WENDOVER, MR.: A tall, fair, slender young American visiting London, whose coat is rather too clear a shade of blue. Although his conversation is not witty and he treats all subjects as equally important, Laura Wing likes him for his innocence, decency and Americanism. He however merely likes her too, so that her panic-striken attempt to extract a proposal of marriage from him on the eve of a family scandal is unsuccessful. Nevertheless his liking is changed to love by the explanations of a mutual friend Lady Davenant; fired by her account of Laura's heroism and sufferings in her uncomfortable situation, he sets out to win her by long and diplomatic courtship. *A London Life*

WENTWORTH, CATHERINE: *see* Young, Mrs. Catherine

WENTWORTH, CHARLOTTE: Elder daughter of Mr. Wentworth, thin, pale, with dark smooth hair and quick, bright but calm eyes. She regards her sister Gertrude's imagination and unpredictability with admiration and anxiety, and heroically suppresses her own love for Gertrude's suitor Mr. Brand. In her gentleness and dutiful self-sacrifice, she is the pattern of New England womanhood from which Gertrude departs, but Mr. Brand finally recognises her merits and marries her. *The Europeans*

WENTWORTH, CLIFFORD: A slim, mild-faced young man with the neatly arranged features of his father. He talks in a softly growling tone expressing shyness and humour; his manners are very gauche. His suspension from Harvard for a drinking spree worries his father; and his European cousins Felix Young and Eugenia Münster think he should be given polish by a mild flirtation with Eugenia. In fact a conventional and honest boy, only too anxious to renounce dissipation to placate his family, Clifford makes a straightforward, New England rejection of the subtleties of experience Eugenia is offering him, hastily marries his pretty childhood sweetheart Lizzie Acton, and thankfully settles down to his respectable destiny. *The Europeans*

WENTWORTH, GERTRUDE: Mr. Wentworth's younger daughter, a tall, pale, thin, rather awkward young lady of two- or three-and-twenty, with straight fair hair: her strange dark eyes originally look both troubled and dull. Her rebellion against the New England virtues of placidity and self-repression shows in occasional bad temper, of which her suitor Mr. Brand hopes to cure her. However the arrival of her European cousins Eugenia Münster and Felix Young reveals a different way of life: they share her reluctance to take pleasures sadly. Her marriage to Felix fortunately frees her strong character and imagination for enjoyment and action. *The Europeans*

WENTWORTH, MR. WILLIAM: A tall, lean man of ascetic, even cadaverous appearance, who is gentle and infinitely conscientious. This, and his very earnestness, make it difficult for him to judge people and situations; he is both fascinated and bewildered by his European niece and nephew Eugenia Münster and Felix Young, whose assumptions are so alien from his own, though with the liberality that is his only pride he loans them a house for their visit. He remains bewildered as the young people around him pair off according to unperceived emotional currents rather than as he rationally expects. *The Europeans*

WESTGATE, MR. J. L.: A tall, lean personage with a thin, sharp, familiar face, quick intelligent eye, thick brown moustache and sociable but business-like expression. Works very hard at his business in New York while his wife spends the summer in cooler Newport: there he sends Lord Lambeth and Percy Beaumont, introduced by a mutual friend. *An International Episode*

WESTGATE, MRS. KITTY: An extremely pretty woman whose manner and intelligence are sharper if less deep than her sister Bessie Alden's. She warns Bessie against appearing too anxious for the company of Lord Lambeth, but when she learns that her sister does not love him, she encourages her to 'frighten' his noble family by seeming likely to marry him—mainly to revenge herself for various slights from English society. *An International Episode*

WHITEFOOT, MR.: A young Orthodox minister, invited to Roderick Hudson's farewell picnic party, where his increasing conversational sonority foreshadows his conversion to episcopy twelve months later. *Roderick Hudson*

WHITEROY, LORD: Eldest of the seven brothers of Lord Frederick Purvis. He and his family do not believe Lord Frederick, stabbed to death by Florentine Vivier, is the father of her child Hyacinth Robinson. *The Princess Casamassima*

WHITEROY, LADY: Nick Dormer does not attend her house party at Severals as he promised, considering the probable opportunities for meeting Julia Dallow there will be more provoking than satisfactory. *The Tragic Muse*

WHITESIDE, MRS.: Aunt of Mr. Wentworth, who takes his half-sister Catherine to Europe. It is her lamentable account of the husband Catherine finds there that chills family feeling and effects Catherine's estrangement. *The Europeans*

WINDRUSH, LADY: Mother of Peter Sherringham and Julia Dallow, cousin of Lady Agnes Dormer. *The Tragic Muse*

WING, LAURA: A young American girl, who has lived since her parents' impoverishment and death with her married sister Selina Berrington. Her lack of income, her attachment to her sister and her sense of duty keep her with Selina after she becomes aware of her loveless, abusive marriage and dangerously reckless social life. Unsuccessful in her constant appeals to Selina, though deceived for a while by her pretence of repentance and reformation, Laura is shattered by her sister's sudden elopement with a lover, carried out deliberately in the most public and offensive way. In the stress and panic of the moment Laura tries to extract a proposal of marriage from her American admirer Mr. Wendover, and in the reaction of shock and shame becomes quite ill. Nevertheless she pursues Selina for one last appeal, and is next heard of returning to America to take refuge with some distant cousins. The newly ardent Mr. Wendover follows her for a long, diplomatic courtship. Though her moral sensitivity resists the influence of expediency, complacency and powerlessness, she suffers unnecessarily from feeling implicated in Selina's wrongdoing. *A London Life*

WINKWORTH, MISS: Henry Burrage is falsely rumoured to be engaged to her. *The Bostonians*

WINTERBOURNE, FREDERICK: A young American of seven-and-twenty who has been at school and college in Geneva, where he now lives. His long exile from America makes him unfit to judge the traveller Daisy Miller's behaviour: his first and correct impression that she is simple and ignorant of European conventions is undermined later by her stubborn frequentation of the young Italian Giovanelli's company. Meeting them at the Colosseum by moonlight, Winterbourne thinks and says that Daisy is not virtuous, but her pathetic denials during her subsequent fatal illness convince him that he is mistaken, and has failed a test of his own understanding. *Daisy Miller*

WIX, CLARA MATILDA: Mrs. Wix's little daughter, who has been knocked down and killed on the spot by a hansom cab. *What Maisie Knew*

WIX, MR.: The one person in Mrs. Wix's life about whom she does *not* endlessly talk to her pupil Maisie. He has been dead 'for ages'. *What Maisie Knew*

WIX, MRS.: An ugly, odd, poor woman, whose 'divergent obliquity of vision' is corrected by glasses she calls 'straighteners'. Her once yellow hair, now a greasy sad grey, is dressed in unfashionable braids and dingy bun, and her one snuff-coloured dress is glazed with antiquity. However her cross, beetle-like appearance is deceptive for she is warm-hearted, sentimental and loyal. Engaged as governess to Maisie Farange she teaches little, but supplies what is available nowhere else—motherliness. Safer than anyone else in the world, her safety—rather than her conventional morals—is the standard by which Maisie's more beautiful but volatile parents and stepparents are found wanting. Thus Maisie chooses to confide herself to Mrs. Wix when neither Sir Claude nor Mrs. Beale, her stepfather and stepmother, will sacrifice each other for Maisie's sake. *What Maisie Knew*

WOODLEY, WILLIE: The gentlest, softest young man it is possible to meet, an American known as 'the best dancer in the world'. He knows a great deal about England and is considered by Mrs. Westgate as a respectable escort for her sister Bessie Alden. *An International Episode*

WRIGHT, GORDON: Longueville's excellent honest friend, with clear grey eyes, short straight flaxen hair and irregular features that gain grace from a powerful yellow moustache. He tends to take everything seriously, but Longueville's unfavourable opinion of Angela Vivian does not deter him from proposing marriage. He greets her refusal with some relief, but later, tiring of the naïve simplicity for which he has married Blanche Evers, he seeks out Angela again and regards her engagement to Longueville (who has changed his mind) as base treachery. The tactful Angela guesses that he really loves his wife, convinces him of Blanche's love, and restores him to sanity and happiness. *Confidence*

X

X, PRINCESS: A good-natured princess, at whose ball in Rome Nora Lambert makes her début. *Watch and Ward*

Y

YOUNG, MR. ADOLPHUS: Father of Eugenia Münster and Felix Young. Born in Sicily of American parents, he is regarded as a lamentable foreigner by his bride's family. *The Europeans*

YOUNG, MRS. CATHERINE: Older half-sister of Mr. Wentworth, she visits Europe when twenty never to return. She makes a wilful and undesirable marriage there, which she neither regrets nor apologises for: her family thereafter ignore her. *The Europeans*

YOUNG, FELIX: An inveterately happy young man, strictly more handsome than his sister Eugenia Münster, whom he accompanies to America to meet their Wentworth cousins. Born in France, by the age of twenty-eight he has wandered all over France and Germany performing in travelling bands of actors and musicians, or paying his way, as he intends to do in America, by his slight but talented portraits and sketches. Pleased by everything, his first delight in the American girls becomes love for one, his cousin Gertrude Wentworth. His nature is 'intrinsically joyous' and he measures his own healthy good intentions only by their practical effect, so that, unlike the Wentworths, he is not tormented by spiritual aspirations or introspection, nor, like his sister, by material or social ambition. Though never 'serious' he is honest because of his disinterestedness, and trustworthy in his sense and experience, and at last persuades the Wentworths to let Gertrude marry him: they lead the changeful but untroubled wandering life which suits him. *The Europeans*

Animals and Other Non-Human Characters

BUNCHIE: A little rowdyish, bristling, bustling terrier belonging to Ralph Touchett. *The Portrait of a Lady*

LISETTE: Maisie Farange's French doll, on which she practises the airs of mystery and superiority that adults practise on her. *What Maisie Knew*

STENTERELLO: Christina Light's poodle, which goes everywhere with her. *Roderick Hudson*

NOTE

Several name changes occur in the various editions of James's work, particularly in the New York Edition. For this reason, the following appendix notes the New York Edition variants in italic.

The Characters—Book by Book

The Ambassadors

The American

The American (cont.)

The Aspern Papers

The Awkward Age

The Bostonians

Confidence

Daisy Miller: A Study

The Europeans

The Golden Bowl

An International Episode

In the Cage

A London Life

The Other House

The Portrait of a Lady

The Portrait of a Lady (cont.)

The Princess Casamassima

The Princess Casamassima (cont.)

The Reverberator

Roderick Hudson

Roderick Hudson (cont.)

The Sacred Fount

The Spoils of Poynton

The Tragic Muse

The Tragic Muse (cont.)

The Turn of the Screw

Washington Square

Watch and Ward

What Maisie Knew

The Wings of the Dove